12 THINGS EVERY PARENT SHOULD KNOW

IRENE BANGWELL

Published in Nigeria by
Handz and Mindz Ltd
P.O. Box 8531,
Wuse, Abuja
Nigeria

First Edition
First Printing, 2019

ISBN: 978-9-7897-2422-2

Cover Design
Vodina West
Lakitha Munasinghe

DEDICATION

This book is dedicated to every parent who is determined to shape this generation for a great future.

Toast to all of us.

IRENE BANGWELL

IRENE BANGWELL

BOOK MAP

Dedication iii
Book Map v
Acknowledgement vii
Foreword ix
Introduction: It's a new city 1

#1 Change is Imminent 9

#2 The Age of the Working Mum 11

#3 Competitive Value System:
Non-parental care givers 23

#4 Competitive Value System: Internet,
Technology & Devices 35

#5 Education in the 21st century. 57

#6 The rise and rise of attention seeking
behavior and social media addiction. 69

#7 The new narrative on love, sex and marriage. 77

#8 The 'woke' generation 89

#9 The 21st century family structure 101

#10 Helping your children find their feet. 113

#11 Communication; The power tool of 21st
century parenting. 127

#12 To spank or not to spank   135

The Crux of the Matter;
Building Emotional Resilience   149

Conclusion   161

ACKNOWLEDGMENTS

Taking up projects such as this requires having the right support system; spiritual support system, family support system, office team and friends who cheer you on.

I have been blessed with the gift of a strong support system and I have a lot to show for it. I took up a couple of writing projects at the same time including the writing of **12 Things Every Parent Should Know** and my support system at every point in time, made it possible.

I also want to appreciate parents who have trusted me over the years with the mentoring of their children and teenagers. Thank you very much for the many learning opportunities you created for me. Thank you for your faith in me.

I would love to specially thank my fathers of faith for all I have learned from them and how these learnings have equipped and shaped me for what God wants of me. I would love to specially appreciate Pastor Andy & Ndidi Osakwe, Drs. Abel & Rachel Damina, Pastor Efezino & Folashade Idheze and Pastors Eshiet & Ofonime Udosen.

I would love to sincerely appreciate, my amazing husband, Kingsley Bangwell. There is no word to describe how blessed I am to have someone who sees what I can be and steadily reminds me to leave my mark in the world. I love you today and always.

I would also love to specially appreciate my brilliant

daughters, Briona and Elena, who made the biggest sacrifice during the time of executing this book writing projects.

Special thanks to my two foster daughters, Anurika Okoli and Rahab Kumbo, who stepped in, as they always do, to watch the girls and the home-front during these times. I pray that God blesses you greatly and raises help for you as you pursue greatness in your time.

To my amazing, brilliant, resourceful assistant, Sharon Ahumibe, I say, step out there, you have what it takes to live out the best version of your life.

When it was time to identify someone to write the foreword of this book, it had to be someone who had already gone through the 21st Century parenting phase; ahead of the rest of us. I wanted feedback that what had been articulated in the book had been tried and tested. This is what Mr. Julius Adeoye brought to fore, having raised three amazing young people, he did justice to the conversation. Thank you, Sir, for your faith and diligence.

Special thanks to my great friends, Bar. Rose Ojabo, Coach Sam Obafemi and Dr. Emmanuel Adegbe for giving of their precious time to review this book. Thank you does not cut it.

Thank you, Valerie Vishnay & Mordecai Gbaratu, for being amazing and wonderful and patient too. Thank you to great friends who lent professional help during these times especially Kaiso Dahnyels and Vodina West.

Thank you to my mum, Odo Bassey Otu and brother, Joshua Essien for their faith in me.

Everyone needs a tag team that believes in them completely and periodically calls them to order, so that one steadily defies the odds and lives out the very best version of their lives. Mine is made up of some of the most amazing people you can imagine. Thank you Mrs. Angela Ajala, Mrs. Olusola Bankole, Emem Opashi, Tina Amachree, Kai Orga, Chidiebube Ocheme, Stephanie Itenebe, Wendy Ologe, Viviann Okoye, Inimfon Etuk, Aruk Eteng, Deborah Ikongbeh and so many other amazing people, thank you for your gift of beautiful friendship.

More than eleven years ago, I was so certain that I needed to write but there wasn't that much clarity of what I was going to write. For starters, I just could not get myself to eventually write. The projects I had started, as passionate as I was, I just couldn't bring myself to finish. Till date many of them remain unfinished.

Then Grace happened! Taking me totally on a different journey and pathway than I could ever have thought or imagine. Unprecedented.

Four published works, two manuscript and two outlines later, I have come to return all the glory and honor to the King. Yes, to the maker of times, seasons, graces and places. The one who created me for His own good pleasure, glory and purpose.

Every single thought, insight, knowledge, you would find in these pages are God-breathed. He created all of the events from which I came to draw insights and meaning from.

The strongest memory I have throughout these writing projects is putting pen to paper and just finding words pour out in dimensions I have never thought about. At the weirdest of places and in very awkward moments, I have felt the urge to write and then it just poured out.

I have experienced a divine phenomenon.

This is the Father's time for these learnings. It's been a privilege being a part of this experience.

To the King of Kings and the Lord of Lords, I return ALL of the glory.

Irene Bangwell
Abuja, Nigeria
April 2019

FOREWORD

It is easier to build strong children than to repair broken men.
- Frederick Douglass

Frederick Douglass could not be more correct in making that statement. There's a whole lot that goes into raising children. The journey is such a dynamic one in which you keep learning all the way. I found out that the number of children you have would almost always determine the number of approaches you would employ in dealing with them, and it may even be a combination of many rapidly evolving styles at that.

This book, for me, is like a re-awakening or careful attempt to draw us into the current realities on parenting in this day and age. Just as the world around is changing rapidly and adapting to new developments, new innovations, technological breakthroughs, artificial intelligence AI, internet and internet of things, so also are our children and everyone else. While this is going on all around us, we cannot afford to play the, proverbial, 'ostrich' and expect to stubbornly live in the past.

12 Things Every Parent Should Know - 21st Century Parenting is a book you will love to read. The book is easy to read, easy to understand and identify with. It is a compendium of real - life parental issues that many people grapple with on a daily basis. It is well presented with a genial flavor, very honest personal examples, a bit of humor, and seriousness all at the same time.

This book is timely. It is designed to be every parent's companion. It is not a novel or ordinary storybook; it is a working manual for every parent who desires to build a strong child that would give them rest and peace of mind in old age.

My wife and I have been parents for about 21years, we are blessed with 3 beautiful children, in spite of all the years of experience, I have learnt new things from this book. There are so many things I took for granted and a lot in which I was fortunate to have done the right thing back then, even though it wasn't as if I knew much about parenting at the time. Call it "beginner's luck" and you would be spot-on.

The insights shared by Mrs. Bangwell in this compilation of 12 strategic parenting nuggets are very much applicable to every parent, irrespective of the age of your children and your beliefs.

I particularly love the way she took us through the journey of how the society has evolved from the time we were growing up in small towns or villages and then on to this present dispensation with gadgets everywhere. It filled me with nostalgia and got me laughing at some of the examples which I readily identified with.

I would like to mention that the intention of this book and the author is definitely not to throw out everything we know about parenting as we 'inherited' it from our parents through the windows. Absolutely not! Rather it is an attempt at presenting parenting to us from the standpoint of a 21st century child so that we could be better equipped at raising global leaders.

After reading this book, you will start approaching parenting from an empathic viewpoint which would, most likely, usher in a new season of mutual respect, openness, love and affection between parents and their wards.

It is noteworthy that this 21st century approach to parenting does not seek to indulge the children, neither is it seeking to relegate the role of discipline, seriousness and a sense of responsibility, rather it seeks to be a bridge between different generations. It teaches us to partner with our children to bring out the best in them.

In my own experience with my children who are now young adults, I decided to flow with the trends by preparing myself, mentally, physically and psychologically for about any unexpected demands that may be placed on my parenting skills. I've had to bend on issues that are not too fundamental, I've had to 'play along' on issues that cannot do any harm to anyone.

I've had to 'put down my feet' when it was time to be firm on issues. I've had the opportunity to tell one of my sons, when he needed motivation, that "I would not judge you by someone else's standards, because it would be unfair to judge a fish by its inability to climb a tree" and that helped him through those times.

This book has opened my eyes to more skills that I might adopt in my quest to be a parent worthy of raising strong children.

Julius I. Adeoye
A husband, a father, a marriage counselor
CEO – Aristoclean Limited

IT'S A NEW CITY
(INTRODUCTION)

Saying that parenting today is significantly different from when we were raised is stating the obvious.

What has changed?

What is the nature of this change? Has it changed for good or for bad?

Maybe the change is not in terms of good or bad. Perhaps it's much more in terms of difference. So what is different today?

Are all our parents' approaches to parenting wrong?

Are there things that today's parents can learn from yesterday's parents? Do you consider yesterday's parents – your own parents – to have been successful?

Regardless of your opinion, have you really taken the time to clearly articulate what their successes were and what their relative failures were?

Parenting today is like moving back to the city where you grew up in. Just thinking about this reminds me of Calabar, as I knew it.

What city did you grow up in?

Let us imagine that about two decades have passed between the time you lived there and you have just returned. Imagine that this city has been blessed with fantastic, innovative and growth-driven leaders who have done well in growing the city.

There are probably better roads, stable electricity and there's an avalanche of high-rise buildings as a result of the volume of local and international trade that is carried out in this city today. For one, there are definitely more people in the city from different states and other tribes.

This city you once grew up in is now hugely multilingual with all kinds of new businesses. Yes, from people who are hired to home-school children, to people who go to offices to take measurements for producing custom-made shirts and well-tailored suits delivered within 72 hours. There is just about any kind of business. Think of some random business idea and you would be almost certain that someone is already doing something similar if not the exact same.

This city now has a straight phone line to contact the education ministry, police and all kinds of services. There are now community dashboards that enable you find someone who lives near you when you are up to 200 kilometers away from home, so that you can either share their ride or split fares on taxis which, by the way, you hail from your phone.

This city is different from the times you grew up here. It was a much smaller city and Government was about the only form of business here. School was what it was; you walked down to school. There was little or no distance between the school and where you used to live. You could only use the school bus while going for either an excursion or an inter school competition. The chances of sitting in the school bus were super slim and, in fact, you never made it to join the school bus during the course of your entire education.

So now you are back. But you yourself are not back from the caves. You have lived in other big cities and you have seen the trends. You are not exactly shocked by the changes. You kind of understand the trends and you are excited that it's happening in your city. It's not every day that one gets lucky with development coming to a town near them talk more of your city.

So whether it's giving back you have come back for, or the really lucrative economy makes sense to you, you are back. You are back to the city of your childhood. It holds a lot of memories. You know your way around this city - or so you think.

This city has changed. That seems obvious already but you are about to find out the length, breadth and texture of these changes. First, the weather is going to be super unfamiliar. This is just one of the peripheral changes. You lived here as a child and now perhaps you are coming back as a parent with your spouse as well. So your daily routine in this city is going to be from a totally different perspective.

First, you walked this town as a child, so distances that appeared really long to you as a child are going to now seem a lot shorter to you. Secondly, this city has so changed that the streets are named differently. More so, they are better navigated by landmarks; yes, new landmarks that are unfamiliar to you. Thirdly, the value system has changed. While growing up most people in your everyday life were cousins, neighbors, cousins of neighbors and neighbors of cousins.

Now, there are new faces, languages and therefore newer belief systems. These new people come from other places where they had their own cultures. And the thing with culture is that in the end, it is all about perspective. What is gross in one may be totally acceptable in another.

So, when they mix, it's the perfect recipe of culture-shock ridden chaos. Yes, everyone is now used to it except you - the 'newbie' neighbor. You are even shocked that you could ever be called a 'newbie' here. This is your home! Nah! This used to be your home but there is a new sheriff in town and your name does not ring a bell, just like his name does not ring a bell which really used to be the kind of stuff that was synonymous with your childhood days.

When you would watch TV and when names were called, there was always someone in the room who knew the person, went to school with the person or was friends with the cousin of the person. But, guess what? Names still ring a bell and now it's not around going to school together; it's just about 'knowing' the person. Yes, now people just know people.

They do not necessarily need to have gone to school or have even met with the person.

And finally, the perspective of being a parent means that you will need to find places that was your parent's business to find and they may not have taught you a lot about those aspects of life. Your itinerary now requires you to go through routes that are outside of school, church or mosques.

These would be business routes, unwinding routes and if your economic status has changed from what it used to be when you were growing up, so will your intellectual demands and priorities also have changed so that you will need to find your way differently in this city.

You are in for a culture-shock no matter which way you choose to look at it. However, the better prepared you are for this journey, the more quickly you will get over the shock.

12 Things Every Parent Should Know is like your navigation guide about this new city called 'Parenting in the 21st Century'. You were raised by parents, you are familiar with how they raised you and now you have become a parent but the perspectives and parenting realities have dramatically changed.

There will be bumps no matter what but there will be a lot fewer bumps when you are better prepared. And if you feel like you can bulldoze your way through this city, get ready. You may lose money, miss your way, waste time, hurt yourself and maybe even hurt your little ones.

This 'parenting' business requires new knowledge, skills, values and attitudes but the possibilities are more than you can ever imagine. You have to be willing to learn parenting. Following your gut instinct sounds super cool, but your instinct can just be your old self trying to find its way in the city it assumes it knows. You cannot count on it.

Super parents, put on your beach shirt and top, nice

sunglasses and whatever else makes you feel comfy (this city's new word for comfortable), step into my boat and let's get this cruise started!

The contents in this book should make you laugh, smile, tense you up a bit but show life hacks to help navigate your way through this city.

My name is Irene Bangwell. It's a rare privilege to be your tour guide.

#1 CHANGE IS IMMINENT

Not all change has to be viewed with trepidation. I love this quote by Andrew Smith which says that "People fear what they do not understand and hate what they cannot conquer." When things begin to seem to look all different around you, find what the cause of the change is. Find what is fuelling it and what it is being directed at.

Where there is no change, there would be no growth. In so many ways, the growth is coming from our attempt to solve some of our past problems.

Think of our first experience seeing un-bottled water. It was packaged in flimsy nylon bags that were also used to package saccharine ice creams. Someone thought through it and may have had concerns about the health implication of the general population drinking widely unsupervised and most likely unsafe water.

Imagine that they brainstormed and came up with the new way of packaging water that was designed to be safe and serve a market made up of people who could not afford the bottled water.

This new package would now come to be supervised for its safety for consumption by agencies like National Agency for Food and Drugs Administration and Control (NAFDAC), thus making a huge difference in the state of our health. This brought change, this brought growth.

As parents, the changes around us are not all bad. In many cases, they are there to help us solve existing problems.

Let's explore some of the most remarkable changes that have come with the 21st century.

- **Key Point**

- Throughout the course of your life as a parent, so many more things are likely to change right before your eyes. Seek to understand what need the changes are there to meet, and then take a stand or make the necessary adjustments.

#2 AGE OF THE WORKING MUM

The 21st century is largely characterized by two parents working in one formal setting or the other. What it means to be a mum, for example, has changed dramatically in the last century. Debates for and against the woman's decision to either be a stay at home mum by her volition, or work outside of their home either on a full time or part time basis are on-going but we do not anticipate any remarkable changes coming up any time soon.

Traditional family settings were previously characterized by a man who, as the leader of the home, took responsibility for everything that revolved around finance. He was primarily the one who worked outside of the home while the wife was responsible for looking after the children and keeping the home. Roles have changed dramatically; many of these changes have been induced by events and circumstance that required a change in strategy.

During wars, for instance, many men were required to go fight in the army leaving a vacuum for which women rose up to fill. Situations of job losses, ill health and even death of a husband have contributed to the changing face of parental roles and responsibilities.

The above-mentioned factors have not been the only factors responsible for women taking up jobs; the other factors include women's attainment of higher educational levels, and families' decision to explore better standards of living that require resources to be pooled together to meet family needs.

There have also been grounds of women taking up employment so that they could earn their own money. For many, this has been for personal fulfillment while for others it has really been about personal security. In the event where a husband was oppressive, divorced them without notice or where they were in a domestic violence situation, it served as a backup for starting life over.

For many women, watching their mothers not pursue their life's goals has been the impetus to not end up like she did. Yes, there has generally been dissatisfaction at oppressive models where women were compelled to stay at home. Most women today want to have a say in whether or not they stay at home.

Not also forgetting the fact that the 21st century has been synonymous with conversations and realization that everyone has been created to fulfill a purpose, and is embedded with gifts and talents.

Finally, many women have taken up paid employment prior to even getting married because of the burden of taking responsibility for family members including sick parents, and providing for the education of their siblings. All of these narratives go to show that there are several legitimate grounds for more women showing up, alongside their male counterparts, at the workplace.

While this is the new order, this change has had a lopsided effect on things. While women embrace formal work, their male counterparts have not really embraced the housekeeping roles.

You would expect that with shared contributions to finances (hopefully women are as responsive), there would be a corresponding sharing of household responsibilities. Rather, alternative measures to addressing housekeeping roles are put in place.

All of these have created a whole new reality for parenting in the 21st century in terms of how parents are carrying out their primary responsibility of caregiving to their children.

Here is a look at some of the outcomes of this new

work structure;

Less and less parents are supervising their children

While we were growing up, there was always one of the parents at home or the grand parent who could easily identify when a child was up to some mischief. Today's children close from school, get home and have enough time and space to experiment on very dangerous things. Most of the helps at home are not well educated and so the children can outsmart them.

There are conversations speaking for the significant role played by grandparents of the past and its impact on the overall wellbeing of children. Many grandparents today are still in the working class and therefore unable to support like in times past.

There are lower and lower moral standards

From the point of waking up, to the time of getting to sleep, they are passed on from one person to another. In many cases there is not a firm enough moral standard to follow.

Parents come home fatigued

Parents are always tired and so they look away from habits and behaviors that should be of concern but the fatigue does not allow them process as quickly.

Many times, habits escalate and become real causes for concern. Even when parents identify a cause for concern, there is not enough time to think through it or the strength to consistently follow through an action plan that should help.

There is not enough room for conversations, fostering relationships, answering questions and making clarifications.

Children can pick up the wrong belief and grow up with it without parents even having an inkling it's there. The absence or very sporadic patterns of conversations allows us talk over their heads and reel out instructions every now and then. Sometimes we feign being strict just to come out as firm and disciplinarians but this does not have the follow through of steady conversation because we are not always home.

The guilt of working long hours makes us as parents try to bribe our children with everything.

Many parents say that they want to give their children what their own parents never gave them. In the first instance, I realized later in life that our parents surely gave us the best they could with what they knew and resources that were available to them.

Also, even if you were able to give your children what they didn't give you, chances are that's not all your children need. And for each child, what they need is different. So, it's possible that your children may not really need what you needed when you were younger.

While this does not invalidate every effort you are making to be a better parent, it just means you should be intentional about giving your children what they really need for the context of today's reality.

The guilt of work is making us give in too soon, be permissive, use gifts and toys as a bribe for our time.

In summary, today there is a lot less supervision of children over longer hours by their own parents. Parents - mothers and fathers alike - work longer hours and take very demanding responsibilities that leave them fatigued at the end of the day. The fatigue they feel blurs their judgment.

Today's parents are offering less and less listening ears, answering less and less questions. Parents are demanding standards that they do not effectively teach and model. As a result, as parents, we are not giving children the support they need age after age. This in turn has induced critical changes that characterize the 21st century, one of which is children's continual search for validation in places and people outside of their parents.

There are also a number of us who are too nonchalant about how much impact our absence has on our children and for many of us, we throw around the fact that our parents weren't emotional towards us. Some of us say, "Our parents didn't do this or that and we didn't die." My response would usually be, "Is it possible that there could have been a different and perhaps even better version of you?" Is it possible that your parents didn't know better but now you know?

12 Things Every Parent Should Know is written to help every parent become aware of what our parenting responsibilities are in the 21st century. Your parents may have gotten away with how they raised you because they weren't raising a 21st century child but you are. And that is what matters.

What can a parent do to manage this?

1.   The first step is to try guilt-free parenting. Take responsibility for your absence. But know that your child is not the boss of you. If you were unavoidably absent, apologize but do not beg. You do not need to beg because this is very likely going to be the boat your children would soon find themselves in. So, part of your role is to show them how to create work-life balance.

When you get home after missing say a school activity (hopefully, you are not habitually absent), move on to ask what happened when you were away. Drop your phone down and show genuine interest in their school activity. Let them see you really mean to be there. Please do not bully your children.

Some parents use this route as an escape from the guilt. Do not make it sound like you went to work for them so they should shove their expectations. Love is the reason why they expect you around. They love your company. Know that it would not last through your lifetime. So do not abuse it.

2.   This is not the "do as I say" generation. This is the "buy in" generation. Since you would not always be at home, instilling values needs to be at core where your child develops a conviction about what it is you are trying to teach them. This is the communication-based generation. Answer the "WHYS" and help them develop a rock-solid foundation on different issues.

Have an open door policy. Let them be free to tell you what happened at school or during your absence including their own misbehavior. That way, you can pull out teachable moments from events that happened even in your absence.

When you see something that is wrong the first time and every other time, correct the children. Remind them of what the standards are and if there are natural consequences or logical consequences, please follow through.

3. Since you already work during the week, reduce the weekend engagements you sign up for. You cannot eat your cake and have it. Have a well laid out plan on activities you plan to do with the children. Please create

family traditions that you do together with the children. Make memories with your children.

Some families can plan for the fathers to do pick-up on Fridays and during their drive home they do fun stuff like doing some karaoke and essentially catching up.

I find that so many fathers today do not believe there is a way that this can be woven into their already full schedules and I recommend starting with the "identity" you want your children to have about you.

Stewart Friedman in his Harvard Business Review article titled "How Our Careers Affect Our Children" states that "children were more likely to show behavioral problems if their fathers were overly involved psychologically in their careers, whether or not they worked long hours. And a father's cognitive interference of work on family and relaxation time — that is, a father's psychological availability, or presence, which is noticeably absent when he is on his digital device — was also linked with children having emotional and behavioral problems.

For mothers, on the other hand, having authority and discretion at work was associated with mentally healthier children. That is, we found that children benefit if their mothers have control over what happens to them when they are working. Further, mothers spending time on themselves — on relaxation and self-care — and not so much on housework, was associated with positive outcomes for children.

It's not just a matter of mothers being at home versus at work, it's what they do when they're at home with their non-work time. If mothers were not with their children so they could take care of themselves, there was no ill effect on their children. But to the extent that mothers were engaged in housework, children were more likely to be beset by behavior problems.

4. Your rest is a priority. Take out activities that steal out of your rest time like excessively spending time on social media, staying up late into the night, etc. Invest some level of commitment to your rejuvenation. And do well to read my book **'Moving from Overwhelmed to Overwhelm'.**

Always have it at the back of your mind that the children are not here to drain you. So, you should make the time to rest. Also know that when you spend time playing and in conversation with the children, it rejuvenates you and as such is mutually fulfilling for you and the children.

5. There is an age your children get to and you may need to tone down on travels if your job demands that. There are responsibilities you may not be able to take on at work when your children are in the pre-puberty stage. This is the truth. You cannot completely eat your cake and have it.

Should you need to take a step back, please do not feel guilty or mediocre about such measures. Rid yourself as well of the 'fear of missing out'. Hopefully corporate organizations, can design departments that allow both parents work maximally, rise through the ranks without sacrificing their children's wellbeing. There should be provision for working remotely when there is a need to.

The 21st century call to better, stronger and more effective parenting is a national emergency. We are losing our children - both those here at home and those in the diaspora - to drugs and all kinds of vices. Nothing will replace our role in their lives.

If it takes five years to switch roles and come back in when the children are stable, consider it an investment in your retirement. These things catch up and stay with us long after the corporate world closes the curtain on us.

Let's make taking care of the children cool again. Let's make nice T-shirts with the inscription "I spent the weekend with the children". Let's produce ads that do not only show that we are putting aside money for the children. Let the adverts also show parents eager to go meet with the children at the close from work.

We are the generation that can create and tweak. We are the generation that must change career and parenting from being the question of either or to things we can do together and well. We can do this. Let's do this.

6.   Give third party legitimacy to supervise your children. First and foremost, if possible, have at least one domestic staff that speaks English fairly well. Talk to the domestic staff with respect so that your children continue to see them as authority figures.

This is an entire 21st century dynamic, so I have dedicated an entire chapter in this book to third party value systems and all the shenanigans that come with it.

- Key Points

- There is a need for both parents to share in performing parenting responsibilities.
- In the 21st century, achieving work-life balance is extremely important.
- We must forge strong bonds of trust and relationships within our families.

#3 COMPETITIVE VALUE SYSTEM: NON-PARENTAL CAREGIVERS

The average 21st century child starts some form of education or school-based care by the time they are three months old. In times past, here in Nigeria, children only started school when their left hand could go over their head to touch their right ear. Not so today. With three months only **for maternity** leave and the millennial grandma who is equally working, many families do not have someone close to home, staying back to watch the new born baby. For many families, a crèche is a safer option than leaving the child with a total stranger at home.

No matter what option is preferred: crèche or home care, from 3 months old, babies begin to interact with minders, nannies, caregivers, etc. who are often referred to as non-parental caregivers.

I personally believe that it is not the same as parental care but research, such as those adopted by organizations such as Psychology Today, shows that day-care has a variety of measurable effects, many of them positive and some of them negative. And they hinge on the quality of the care, the type of care, and the amount of time spent in it, pretty much as with parenting.

Researchers now know that the nature of day-care arrangements (more than ten hours a week spent in the care of someone other than the mother) has a long reach.

The type and quality of care can influence many aspects of development—including memory, language development, school readiness, math and reading achievement, the nature of relationships with parents and teachers, social skills, work habits, and behavioral adjustment—at least through grade school. That's important because in many domains, patterns established by the third grade or primary three as in the case in Nigeria, tend to become highly stable and enduring.

Recently, a new wave of results was released and made news because they confirmed and bolstered the validity of an earlier finding that day-care is associated with some negative effects on child behavior.

not be family members to undertake
baby, which eventually goes on to be
time our children start school. Many
caregivers may live with us.

ing is that usually, the only people we
ing in to our families to care for the
ays most likely to be poorly educated,
xperience taking care of children and,
earning on the job. The very fact that
on the job is usually the first point of

rhaps mothers most especially, we
d before we know it, we become easily
nese people and resent them. Our
ow we speak with them and place a

these **people** are unable to get our
p to the standards. Depending on how
one disrespecting such people, your
you up against each other which all
atever efforts they could have put in
r absence.

overwork these people and this leaves
ut and disconnected as we would be
y undermining the role they could

The study found that the more time a child spent in center-based day-care before kindergarten, the more likely their sixth-grade teacher was to report that the child "gets in many fights," is "disobedient at school," and "argues a lot."

Beverley Amsel in her 2013 article, "The Effects of Parental Involvement on Self-Confidence and Self-Esteem" puts it most brilliantly as captured below:

"Very early in life, parents' responsiveness to their babies affects the development of self-confidence and self-esteem. It takes little effort to summon a picture of a doting parent responding to a baby with loving noises, engaged chattering, focused attention, and cuddling. Baby smiles, parent smiles back. As the infant matures, parents continue to respond and mirror what the baby is doing. Parental mirroring through early childhood, adolescence, and young adulthood communicates acceptance, acknowledgement, and admiration. This contributes significantly to the development of self-esteem and self-confidence. When parental involvement is limited, children typically receive scant mirroring or encouragement. They have no one reflecting back to them that they are worthwhile, admirable, or interesting."

While both researches apply to the United States of America where day-care centers are tightly regulated and babies spend between 15 - 33 hours each week, the Nigerian context is different. Our standards of day-care are not nearly as regulated for safety, trainings, etc. as in America. Today's parents even opt in for weekend and even boarding crèche services.

In summary, based on various findings as reported again by Psychology Today, here is a real picture of the highs and lows of day care. The lows are to help parents identify areas they need to be proactive about at home.

"Among the varied findings to date:

Memory: Children who spent more time in center-based care displayed an early advantage. They tended to score higher on standardized tests of short-term memory. This effect emerged even before starting school and is maintained during the primary grades.

Cognitive development: Sensitive and responsive care-giving leads to academic achievement throughout the primary grades, as measured by tests of math, reading, and such cognitive processes as memory for sentences.

Social skills: Early positive effects of high-quality care on cooperation, assertion, responsibility, and self-control seemed to disappear at later ages—although the researchers point out that long-term positive effects on social development may well reappear at a later age because development is dynamic.

Behavior problems: Even high-quality care did not reduce the number of behavior problems among those

in childcare.

Conflictual re
based child-ca
parents and te

Work habits:
spent in chil
teachers late
independentl
not complete

Social-emotic
with peers a
them was ne
care."

After day-car
the efforts
development
and develoj
ourselves tha
can do in sha

These caregi
many times
beyond our
maximize w
present in o

All of this,
narrative. Tl

that may or ma
the caring for t
the pattern by t
of these kinds

1. The first fin
can afford to l
children are alv
have no prior
in many cases,
they are learnin
contention.

As parents, p
correct overly a
irritable **with**
children watch
value on them.

In our absence
children to live
far you have g
children can se
waters down w
supervising in o

Many times, we
them as fagged
ourselves, there
play.

Many of these folks show up in our homes with very questionable values and beliefs and yes, we have to shape them. And every single day and in every moment, they are steadily upholding or over-riding your family values. In many homes, parents are too busy to even set standards and so these caregivers are even the ones trying to have our children clear the table after eating. As good as that sounds, it should not be the ideal. You should as a parent set the tone for standards and values in your home.

How do we get third parties in our living space to work in sync with us instead of going against us?

Imagine that they are actually going to be assistant parents; strive to instill that consciousness in them.

Organize their work in such a way that it does not leave them drained but enables them to be alert as well. Do not over work them to a place of personal drain daily.

Do not be content with the people in your home just running errands for you. Do as much as possible to influence their personal values and orientation. Strive first to instill the same values you want to see in your children in these caregivers.

In my home, a core value that we have is self/personal responsibility. I have two teenage foster children and I am steadily telling them to take control of their lives by changing what they believe about themselves, what they think, and the actions they take and about expecting the most favorable outcomes out of life.

I demand of them to ask questions when they are not clear while also helping them understand that asking questions does not make you look stupid and in the same breadth, I am pushing them to take initiative. It surely is more complex than it sounds in this paragraph. This is the bottom-line of my work - **shaping them** into people who can uphold my standards.

I do not want them thinking hopelessness around my children. I want them to become persons of values. Valuing their bodies, time, education and living a life of focus and priority.

I do realize that this approach will be easier for some than others but bottom-line, you should be working towards this. My daughters are natural homeworkers, meaning that I hardly ever have to ask them to do homework. When the teens (our foster children) joined our family, I told them and continue to tell them the value of school work.

So, by the time they were the ones with the children immediately after school, they picked up their own books too and the children would also follow suit. This helps us create a model for the children to copy or sustain what we have already taught them.

In the 21st century, you cannot afford to run a home

where your domestic staff or relatives who live with you, have no value for themselves, their bodies, the future, their health and you honestly expect this person to hold on to your own ideals. There would surely be conflict.

I have been telling my two foster daughters that they would become their state governors or at least people of prominence in their state. I am really big on this.

A few years ago, I came home to find that one of my daughters had done a shoddy job with her homework. Apparently, one of my foster children had supervised and gone against my 'no calculator' rule during homework. I had noticed this while signing the communication books in the morning and usually I would go through all of their work.

So, I called her and explained to her why a calculator may save time for an adult but a child would hardly know the processes to do it on their own. I told her what homework is all about - which is that homework was something the children have been taught at school and could afford to work independently with minimal help.

Long story, right? It's how you shape what people believe so that there can be a subsequent corresponding action. Like I said earlier, it sounds easier than reality. It is a constant fight to shape anybody's thinking. Our caregivers have been raised in a different environment and under a different set of circumstances compared with what we are expecting of them. As a result, their pace of picking up may be slow but it's a seed we sow and it will blossom.

I have started reaping the benefits in different aspects of our home life even though we are still doing a lot of teaching.

3. Like I mentioned earlier in the previous chapter, getting helps that you can communicate with makes a difference. Even if not all may be able to speak English, at least at each time have one help who can.

4. I celebrate parents that make the effort to take caregivers for medical test to ascertain their state of health. This is a step in the right direction. Please pay attention to their health. All of this helps build the psyche that they are valuable. Also, when they feel unwell, please pay attention even when you believe its pretense.

5. When you bring in someone that has really disturbing behavior, please take the liberty to send them back to their homes or send them to a therapist which may help jump start whatever else you want to do with them. Until you are ready to be available and commit the time needed to shaping their values, then you should not have someone with disturbing behavior around your children.

6. As you create standards at home, demand the same

The study found that the more time a child spent in center-based day-care before kindergarten, the more likely their sixth-grade teacher was to report that the child "gets in many fights," is "disobedient at school," and "argues a lot."

Beverley Amsel in her 2013 article, "The Effects of Parental Involvement on Self-Confidence and Self-Esteem" puts it most brilliantly as captured below:

"Very early in life, parents' responsiveness to their babies affects the development of self-confidence and self-esteem. It takes little effort to summon a picture of a doting parent responding to a baby with loving noises, engaged chattering, focused attention, and cuddling. Baby smiles, parent smiles back. As the infant matures, parents continue to respond and mirror what the baby is doing. Parental mirroring through early childhood, adolescence, and young adulthood communicates acceptance, acknowledgement, and admiration. This contributes significantly to the development of self-esteem and self-confidence. When parental involvement is limited, children typically receive scant mirroring or encouragement. They have no one reflecting back to them that they are worthwhile, admirable, or interesting."

While both researches apply to the United States of America where day-care centers are tightly regulated and babies spend between 15 - 33 hours each week, the Nigerian context is different. Our standards of day-care are not nearly as regulated for safety, trainings, etc. as in America. Today's parents even opt in for weekend and even boarding crèche services.

In summary, based on various findings as reported again by Psychology Today, here is a real picture of the highs and lows of day care. The lows are to help parents identify areas they need to be proactive about at home.

"Among the varied findings to date:

<u>Memory:</u> Children who spent more time in center-based care displayed an early advantage. They tended to score higher on standardized tests of short-term memory. This effect emerged even before starting school and is maintained during the primary grades.

<u>Cognitive development:</u> Sensitive and responsive care-giving leads to academic achievement throughout the primary grades, as measured by tests of math, reading, and such cognitive processes as memory for sentences.

<u>Social skills:</u> Early positive effects of high-quality care on cooperation, assertion, responsibility, and self-control seemed to disappear at later ages—although the researchers point out that long-term positive effects on social development may well reappear at a later age because development is dynamic.

<u>Behavior problems:</u> Even high-quality care did not reduce the number of behavior problems among those

in childcare.

<u>Conflictual relationships:</u> More time spent in center-based child-care led to reports of more conflict—with parents and teacher.

<u>Work habits:</u> The greater the amount of time children spent in childcare in kindergarten, the more their teachers later reported that they do not work independently, did not use their time wisely, and did not complete their work promptly in grade school.

<u>Social-emotional functioning:</u> How skilled children are with peers and how well they solve problems with them was negatively impacted by many hours in day-care."

After day-care, it is our work as parents to complement the efforts of caregivers by fostering behavioral development, independence, problem-solving skills and development. While also steadily reminding ourselves that there is so much caregivers and schools can do in shaping behavior.

These caregivers have to look after several children and many times high-end day-care centers may be well beyond our current financial resources. We have to maximize whatever it is they do by being alert and present in our children's lives.

All of this, by the way, just shows one angle of the narrative. The other option is bringing in third parties that may or may not be family members to undertake the caring for the baby, which eventually goes on to be the pattern by the time our children start school. Many of these kinds of caregivers may live with us.

1. The first finding is that usually, the only people we can afford to bring in to our families to care for the children are always most likely to be poorly educated, have no prior experience taking care of children and, in many cases, learning on the job. The very fact that they are learning on the job is usually the first point of contention.

As parents, perhaps mothers most especially, we correct overly and before we know it, we become easily irritable **with** these people and resent them. Our children watch how we speak with them and place a value on them.

In our absence, these **people** are unable to get our children to live up to the standards. Depending on how far you have gone disrespecting such people, your children can set you up against each other which all waters down whatever efforts they could have put in supervising in our absence.

Many times, we overwork these people and this leaves them as fagged out and disconnected as we would be ourselves, thereby undermining the role they could play.

Many of these folks show up in our homes with very questionable values and beliefs and yes, we have to shape them. And every single day and in every moment, they are steadily upholding or over-riding your family values. In many homes, parents are too busy to even set standards and so these caregivers are even the ones trying to have our children clear the table after eating. As good as that sounds, it should not be the ideal. You should as a parent set the tone for standards and values in your home.

How do we get third parties in our living space to work in sync with us instead of going against us?

Imagine that they are actually going to be assistant parents; strive to instill that consciousness in them.

Organize their work in such a way that it does not leave them drained but enables them to be alert as well. Do not over work them to a place of personal drain daily.

Do not be content with the people in your home just running errands for you. Do as much as possible to influence their personal values and orientation. Strive first to instill the same values you want to see in your children in these caregivers.

In my home, a core value that we have is self/personal responsibility. I have two teenage foster children and I am steadily telling them to take control of their lives by changing what they believe about themselves, what they think, and the actions they take and about expecting the most favorable outcomes out of life.

I demand of them to ask questions when they are not clear while also helping them understand that asking questions does not make you look stupid and in the same breadth, I am pushing them to take initiative. It surely is more complex than it sounds in this paragraph. This is the bottom-line of my work - **shaping them** into people who can uphold my standards.

I do not want them thinking hopelessness around my children. I want them to become persons of values. Valuing their bodies, time, education and living a life of focus and priority.

I do realize that this approach will be easier for some than others but bottom-line, you should be working towards this. My daughters are natural homeworkers, meaning that I hardly ever have to ask them to do homework. When the teens (our foster children) joined our family, I told them and continue to tell them the value of school work.

So, by the time they were the ones with the children immediately after school, they picked up their own books too and the children would also follow suit. This helps us create a model for the children to copy or sustain what we have already taught them.

In the 21st century, you cannot afford to run a home

where your domestic staff or relatives who live with you, have no value for themselves, their bodies, the future, their health and you honestly expect this person to hold on to your own ideals. There would surely be conflict.

I have been telling my two foster daughters that they would become their state governors or at least people of prominence in their state. I am really big on this.

A few years ago, I came home to find that one of my daughters had done a shoddy job with her homework. Apparently, one of my foster children had supervised and gone against my 'no calculator' rule during homework. I had noticed this while signing the communication books in the morning and usually I would go through all of their work.

So, I called her and explained to her why a calculator may save time for an adult but a child would hardly know the processes to do it on their own. I told her what homework is all about - which is that homework was something the children have been taught at school and could afford to work independently with minimal help.

Long story, right? It's how you shape what people believe so that there can be a subsequent corresponding action. Like I said earlier, it sounds easier than reality. It is a constant fight to shape anybody's thinking. Our caregivers have been raised in a different environment and under a different set of circumstances compared with what we are expecting of them. As a result, their pace of picking up may be slow but it's a seed we sow and it will blossom.

I have started reaping the benefits in different aspects of our home life even though we are still doing a lot of teaching.

3. Like I mentioned earlier in the previous chapter, getting helps that you can communicate with makes a difference. Even if not all may be able to speak English, at least at each time have one help who can.

4. I celebrate parents that make the effort to take caregivers for medical test to ascertain their state of health. This is a step in the right direction. Please pay attention to their health. All of this helps build the psyche that they are valuable. Also, when they feel unwell, please pay attention even when you believe its pretense.

5. When you bring in someone that has really disturbing behavior, please take the liberty to send them back to their homes or send them to a therapist which may help jump start whatever else you want to do with them. Until you are ready to be available and commit the time needed to shaping their values, then you should not have someone with disturbing behavior around your children.

6. As you create standards at home, demand the same

behavior from both your children and the domestic staff. Yes, let the same consequence of misbehavior apply. What this means is that the domestic aids will be aware on what the expected standards are, what consequences are and what the standards that have been put in place are to achieve in the first instance.

7. On whether or not there are possibilities of children being misled by domestic staff after all what is said and done, yes, they can. This is why we recommend the measure of catching up on the children and keeping an open-door policy that encourages the children to share what happened including their own misbehavior.

If you run a judgment free atmosphere, both children and domestic staff will not feel like they will be killed when a question of misbehavior comes up. The approach should be a willingness to teach. You could turn this around as a tool and opportunity to help build your children's capacity to refuse to model after standards that parents have clearly spoken against.

- **Key Points**

- We can take our children to crèches but we still have roles to play in shaping their behavior, independence and problem solving skills.
- When we bring in people to live with us, we should strive to shape their own values beyond just having them run errands for us.
- When a person has disturbing behavior, we have the option of sending them away for the sake of their influence on our children.

#4 COMPETITIVE VALUE SYSTEMS: INTERNET, TECHNOLOGY & DEVICES

Just about any 21st century parent you run into tells you about how easily the children of the 21st century operate phones, laptops, etc. Many of them are able to operate these devices **even** before they are able to read.

Most parents relate to this. I guess **that** one of the reasons why mobile devices and screens draw people of all ages, including children, would be that screens appeal to all of our learning styles; the pictures, the sound, the movement or aesthetic. In many ways, it just pulls us in. I see it in my daughters, they hear a sound and they move towards it.

There are two major concerns with the use of technology: the first would be its impact on children's health, and secondly, the role it plays as a third-party value system.

I am talking about an all-encompassing experience that would include the impact of technology and screens on our children's thinking, learning, feelings, behavior, health and wellbeing.

Cary P. Gross once stated that our children are like sponges and we need to remember that they learn from their environment.

In this case what is their environment?

Yale University School of Medicine, National Institutes of Health and California Pacific Medical Centre, through a series of research, determined that on average, today's child spends 45 hours a week with television, movies, magazines, music, the internet, cell phones and video games. By comparison, children spend 17 hours a week with their parents and 30 hours a week in school.

There are research findings showing that overuse of screen technology does more harm than good to our children. Here are some of the findings:

According to The American Academy of Paediatrics, the overuse of screen technology is defined as "the use of screen devices two-plus hours a day for children over the age of two."

TV for Children Filled with Social Bullying

Children aged 2-11 view an alarming amount of television shows that contain forms of social bullying or social aggression.

Physical aggression on television for children is greatly documented, but this is the first in-depth analysis on children's exposure to behaviors like cruel gossiping and manipulation of friendship.

Nicole Martins, Indiana University, and Barbara J. Wilson, University of Illinois, Urbana-Champaign, published in the Journal of Communication a content analysis of the 50 most popular children's shows according to Nielsen Media Research. One hundred and fifty television shows were viewed and analyzed, and 92% of the programming contained some version of social aggression—approximately 14 times per hour. There was careful attention to what was portrayed in the cases of social aggression, whether the behavior was rewarded or punished, justified, or committed by an attractive perpetrator.

The findings suggested that some of the ways in which social aggression is contextualized make these depictions particularly problematic for young viewers.

The study found that attractive characters who perpetrated social aggression were rarely punished for their behavior, and that socially aggressive scenes were significantly more likely than physically aggressive scenes to be presented in a humorous way.

In some cases, social aggression on television may pose more of a risk than portrayals of physical aggression do.

"These findings should help parents and educators recognize that there are socially aggressive behaviors on programs children watch. Parents should not assume that a program is okay for their child to watch simply because it does not contain physical violence. Parents should be more aware of portrayals that may not be explicitly violent in a physical sense but are nonetheless antisocial in nature," Martins said.

If you have a child with a bullying problem, checking what they watch on TV could give you and insight on where to start from. It can be a good place to start the conversations that point to the actions of characters as unacceptable.

Television in children' rooms: Really a bad idea.

Research has long established that for children, more "screen time" is linked to higher rates of obesity. A new study (American Journal of Preventive Medicine) goes further. It finds not only that children with a TV in their

bedroom tend to watch more TV, which in itself

should make them fatter, but also: compared to television watched in, say, a family room, the screen time a child logs in his or her bedroom is linked, hour-for-hour, to more belly fat, higher triglycerides and overall greater risk of developing heart disease and diabetes.

Take two children with roughly the same diet and the same level of physical activity: The study **published** found that the one with a TV in his bedroom (and boys are more likely to have them than girls) will have more cardio metabolic risk factors than the one who has to watch TV in one of his home's common rooms.

The study's lead author, Amanda E. Staiano a researcher with the Pennington Biomedical Research Centre in Louisiana, says "If this gives parents one more bit of ammunition to say, 'No, you cannot have TV in your bedroom,' I'm OK with that." Staiano adds, "If we have fewer obese children in the world, I'll be the Grinch."

Staiano suggested that over and above the effects of being parked too long in front of a TV, a television in the bedroom might magnify the box's corrosive effects on a child's health by disrupting sleep patterns and discouraging the practice of family mealtimes.

Sleep deprivation - the likely outcome when screen time trumps shut-eye - is a known risk factor for obesity and, worse, for metabolic dysfunction. Family mealtimes seem to promote healthier eating and lower obesity rates, not to mention less alcohol, drug and tobacco use by children.

To conduct the study, Staiano and her colleagues studied 369 children and adolescents between 5 and 18 years old. In addition to asking how much television they watched daily and whether they had a TV in their room, the researchers gave the children a battery of tests.

They measured the children' waist circumference, blood pressure and fasting triglycerides; ran a full cholesterol panel; and gauged each child's fat mass in two ways to get precise measures of subcutaneous fat (fat accumulated in the belly and around visceral organs), and overall fat-to-lean mass ratio. And they tested each child's fasting glucose level -- a measure of metabolic function. The researchers also had participants estimate their daily physical activity levels of food intake.

Among children who watched more than two hours of TV a day, those who had a TV in their bedroom were as much as 2 1/2 times likelier than those who did not to be in the top one-quarter of children in terms of fat mass.

That finding held steady even after researchers

adjusted for age, gender, ethnicity, physical activity levels and diet.

Compared to children who had to watch TV in a living area of the home, those who had a TV in their room were almost three times likelier to have "elevated cardio metabolic risk," meaning they had three or more unhealthy readings in the panels of medical tests they were given.

Sheer volume of TV time mattered too: Children who watched five or more hours of TV a day were twice as likely as those who watched less to carry a density of visceral fat that fell in the top quartile.

Sexual Content in Movies May Predict Teen Sexual Behavior

A recent study has found that exposure to sexual content in movies increases the chances of children adopting risky behavior later in life.

"Adolescents who are exposed to more sexual content in movies start having sex at younger ages, have more sexual partners, and are less likely to use condoms with casual sexual partners," said Ross O'Hara, currently a post-doctoral fellow at the University of Missouri, one of the authors of the study, in a statement.

For the study, researchers analyzed sexual content in nearly 684 blockbuster movies between 1998 and 2004.

They found that even movies with G and PG ratings had high levels of sexual content (such as heavy kissing) and that most recent movies do not portray safe-sex methods.

In the second part of the study, they asked 1,228 participants, between the ages of 12 and 14, to report which movie they had seen from a list of 50 randomly selected recent movies. The researchers then conducted a follow-up survey of these participants after 6 years. Participants were asked about their sexual behavior like when they had their first intercourse, use of a contraceptive method, number of sexual partners, etc.

Research has shown that there is a causal effect of sexual content in media on sexual behaviors of adolescents. Other studies have shown that teen-centred films almost always have sexual content in them. Experts say that exposing children to content that is more consistent with actual sexuality can help them think critically about their sexual behavior.

"Much research has shown that adolescents' sexual attitudes and behaviors are influenced by media. But the role of movies has been somewhat neglected, despite other findings that movies are more influential than TV or music," O'Hara said.

Young gamer addicts linked to depression

Children addicted to video games are more likely to suffer depression, anxiety and social phobias and may need professional help to recover, a visiting researcher says.

Once their gaming is back to normal levels, their psychological problems shift, and their mood and school work improve, says Douglas Gentile, a lead researcher on two major studies of video game addiction.

A study of children in the US found nearly one in 10 gamers is a pathological player.

Dr. Gentile, an associate professor in psychology at Iowa State University in his study of 1178 American children found nearly one in 10 gamers to be pathological players and his study of 3034 Singapore youngsters found a similar level of addiction, measured according to standards established for diagnosing gambling addiction.

The pathological gamers in Singapore played 31 hours a week and in the US 20 hours a week but "there was no magic number," Dr. Gentile said.

The measure of pathology was less about the hours youngsters played than the damage gaming was doing to their lives.

The study asked children a series of questions, including whether they ever lied about their gaming, or stole or skipped school to play games; if they felt they could not stop, and if they got anxious and irritable when they tried to stop.

Dr. Gentile said parents had every reason to be concerned if gaming was damaging children's relationships with family and friends, and if their school work was suffering.

"It's a serious problem for some children and they cannot get out of it on their own," he said. "It's not just a phase. In the Singapore study, 84 per cent of those addicted at the start of the study were still addicted two years later and needed professional help to get out of it."

These reports are providing us, evidence-based findings to guide our decision making around these things.

The American Academy Paediatrics (AAP) strongly recommends no television viewing or screen exposure for children younger than two years of age. They stated that when children at any age are fed a diet mainly of virtual world interactions, they are found to:

- Be at risk of developing learning disabilities.
- Have a much harder time dealing with their emotions and feelings.

- Exhibit problem behavior at home and in school.

The Centre for Parenting Education provides some explanations as to why the above listed challenges arise when children are exposed to more than two hours of screen time. In their report, they stated that if a child's growing brain is being fed more than two hours of screen time a day, his brain cannot develop properly.

This can result in:

- A decreased attention span,
- Underdeveloped or delayed language abilities,
- Underdeveloped or delayed critical thinking abilities or creativity skills, and
- Decreased intrinsic motivation for learning.

In addition, they may develop a stimulus addiction and have increased:

- Hyperactivity,
- Aggression,
- Fear,
- Insensitivity, and
- Appetite for violence.

So, what can we do to balance out? What are alternatives to screen use?

1. Flip use of technology.

The primary concern about the overuse of technology is based on the passive pattern of consumption. Children suspend all their sense of reasoning during these screen activities.

To solve this problem, parents can explore other uses of the internet and devices in order to reduce goal less or passive consumption routines.

- Have your children learn creative ways to do math online and afterwards try to practice them.
- Learn arts and crafts that will involve doing something with their hands in order to foster personal learning and creativity.
- Have them learn web building online or coding. Some of the platforms offer these services for free.
- They can take ballet lessons online. The internet allows them to pause, rewind like they would not be able to in a typical classroom.
- They can take enrichment classes online, for example, public speaking.
- They can do research online. You can give them topics to learn about online.
- They can blog by writing, taking pictures or doing Vlogs (Video blogs) that enable them become contributors and not just consumers.
- As we flip the use of the internet, parents must acquaint themselves with effective parental control measures to put in place as their children tow more constructive uses of the

internet while staying within the two hour a day restriction and keeping screens outside of children's bedrooms.

- We should expose our children to the use of devices such as a laptop outside of when it is connected online. They can learn how to use the packages online. Microsoft packages, for instance, can help them develop unique, profitable skills. Many work roles require efficient use of applications such as Microsoft Excel but only a handful of people have the basic skills required to use them.

2. On the use of television screens, let's regulate how many hours our children are just plugged in. The duration spent plus the quality of programs they watch are areas for us to be proactive about. The 21st century allows our children access to a myriad of shows, all round the clock.

Some of these contents come from climes with totally different culture from ours. What is appropriate for a child in a certain place at a certain age may be totally inappropriate here. It will surprise you to know that some things may be overlooked abroad because of the nature of support systems that children have outside of their parents. We cannot stay back in our own country and try to copy the reality of children abroad.

There are all kinds of shows now available from several platforms - terrestrial television, local television, online television, etc.

Parents, too, have content that are specifically designed for them with heavy romantic, violent or diabolical scenes.

These contents are specifically designed for adults because the adult is old enough to make an objective decision regardless of what they may have watched. But it's not the same for children.

A few weeks ago, I read online about a child who kept saying she would poison her teacher and two of her classmates. And people started advising that the child should be prayed for. Not so fast!

We must begin by asking the parents of this what movies she has been watching which are very likely to be inappropriate for her age. Young children are not able to differentiate between entertainment and reality. It doesn't take long for them to come to believe that what they are watching is the reality.

So parents, I am going to ask, what is the PG rating of that telenovela that you are always watching with the children? Have you ever stopped to ask why they have FAM, PG, 13, 16, SNVL inscriptions on different TV shows?

FAM (Family) - Means that the program is suitable for family viewing. Every member of your family can watch the show.

PG (Parental Guidance) - If children are to watch, then parents should be present or guide the entire experience.

13 - When a show is rated 13, it means that the show is not suitable for audiences younger than 13.

16 - When a show is rated 16, it means that the show is not suitable for audiences younger than 16.

S - Means there will be scenes of sex.

N - Means there will be scenes of nudity,

V - Means there will be scenes of violence.

L - Means there will be scenes of strong language. (E.g. use of b** words and f** words and everything in between).

Sometimes I watch a "FAM" show and I literally cringe. Even some cartoons are creepy enough with all the many evil plots, schemes and heavy romance themes, you would be worried, let alone opening up children to adult designed content.

Let's allow our children grow gradually without exposing them to contents that stimulate them sexually and in other very risky ways.

If you also run a business that is patronized by children, please for the sake of their mental health today and in the future, put on TV programs that are healthy enough for them. The adults can manage during those times. Otherwise, have a fixed time for serving children and a time for serving adults. People who run eateries, restaurant and salons should be show more consideration for the children audiences.

Our contemporary music videos are not left out in the category of things that our children should not be exposed to. At children's parties, let's be proactive about sustaining their sanity.

3. What originally made TV, Devices, and the Internet the go to places for our children? We work. We are looking for a means to occupy them while we catch our breath. What other things can we do to keep our children busy other that with devices?

- Let them read. Read to them. Read as a family. Read hardbacks, paper backs, eBooks, and audio books.
- Let them go out and play in the sand. Let them mold.
- Get arts supplies for them to build and play with. Including cardboards, play-doh, water paint, brushes, etc.
- Teach them how to make and fly kites.

- Invest in toys that build their thinking abilities like building blocks, loom band making.
- Help out in the kitchen - boys and girls alike.
- Let them sort laundry.
- Let them go for a walk.
- Buy board games like monopoly, chess, scrabble.
- Let them write stories.
- Buy them puzzle boards.
- Let them play indoor tennis.
- Let them role play together.

There is so much to do to keep the children busy but as a rule of thumb, always ensure that you expose them to experiences that:

- Foster creative thinking.
- Team building.
- Service to others.
- Develop their interest.
- Enables them to express themselves in a healthy way.
- Allows for motion and physical movement.

Whatever you decide to expose your children to should always encompass these six.

4. As your teens get older and use internet the most, you are going to find that the things they read or

watch on social media are going to be a strong influence on them. Early on in life, you have to raise them to ask "says who?" questions and "why?" questions.

Many young people do not realize that social media is open to everyone. Yes, the good, the bad and the ugly. People with all kinds of beliefs, experiences (that color their perspectives) and values included. Apart from that, many people put up posts according to the mood they are in and so they can change their minds pretty quickly, while others post from a position of very limited knowledge.

Help your children learn, early on in life, that they should not believe everything they read. Also let them know that the majority can be wrong. Just because a large number of people are saying something does not always validate it.

Help them to be thinkers. If you have children who ask you questions and sometimes try to argue with you, do not be intimidated by it. Rather, ask them to keep their minds alert as they meet with other people. Ground them with foundational values and principles.

Please avoid being dismissive of your children when they argue. State reasons, facts, experiences and standards to them. Regardless of how they respond, speak with conviction. Then always leave room for both you and them to sleep over issues of debates. Give room for everyone including you to search widely, while stating clearly what sort of sources is considered credible.

The real work is now for you to build conviction for the things you want them to do or not do. For example, why shouldn't they sit directly in front of the TV, why shouldn't they fight, why should they do homework, why should they go to bed on time? Why should there be a curfew?

Arm yourself with reasons. Be prepared. Have conversations. Listen to them. Hear what they have to say. It doesn't mean you are being permissive; it just allows you know where they are coming from. Only from knowing where they are coming from can you safely direct them to where you are.

Think of it this way: imagine that you have a friend visiting you for the first time in your new house. So, you send them the address and while on their way, they miss their way. They call you on the phone but without listening to them, you would not know where they are. Listening to them does not mean you will agree that where they are is your house; it just helps you know how to redirect them to the appropriate destination.

My book **"Raising Children Who Are Influence Proof"** deals elaborately on this.

5. Expose your children to books. Reading helps them gain multiple perspectives to issues. It drives critical reasoning and it's a fuel for creative thinking. Then after that, teach them to question what they read.

6. The 21st century child knows that he is handed devices because his or parents are busy. That really hurts a lot more than parents could ever know. There are times when they are happy they have their devices but there are also times when they NEED your attention.

Let us create family cultures that show that we value each other over devices. Let's model that physical interactions trump technology unless in a context where it is completely unavoidable.

Create no-tech zones at home. For instance, have rules like no phones during meal times, family outings, sitting room times, etc. This will help the whole family unplug from the overwhelm that comes with too much use of devices.

Children and teens regularly use their phones as an escape from the monotonous, boring ways we tend to communicate whenever we go out. Have a caveat for when corrective feedback is meted out. Please do not turn every single outing to an opportunity to state your expectations.

During outings, allow the children to sometimes drive the conversation so that it becomes something they are looking forward to. Essentially de-incentivize their hanging out on their phones. Let them see beyond the rules. Let them see the value.

The 21st century child as a result of the addiction and over use of screens and devices has a very low resilience quotient. They are easily mentally fatigued and harassed. Research shows that 1 in every five children is depressed with suicide rates increased by up to 100% in children aged 10-14 according to FaithIt.

These children are committing suicide over comments on social media and some are possibly misinterpreting their reality. They come on social media and believe that other people have it absolutely better. They would know and believe differently if we spent time talking and talking with them. Yes, if they could come to ask and share their misunderstandings.

7. I recommend that we begin to put our children in pro-social experiences, such as volunteering, visiting families (have them plan the visit and everything that will be needed including food and gifts), holiday jobs, etc. Things that put them in situations where they serve others and take their eyes off themselves while learning about how life is, for most people, helps them straighten out.

Teens who associate very often with adults begin to learn and make far better decisions than teens that were stuck with only their peers.

- Key Points

- It is recommended that children should not spend more than 2 hours on TV or in front of a screen.
- Studies show that children are picking up violent tendencies, adopting risky sexual behaviors from TV shows and movies they watch.
- We have to explore healthier and more productive ways of using both internet and devices.
- There are several healthy ways to keep children busy. We must always think about the potential impact, of whatever it is we give them to keep busy, has on their mental and physical well-being.

#5 EDUCATION IN THE 21ST CENTURY

The very first observation about education in the 21st century would be a steady decline in academic performance which is also now contending with whether or not educational certificates are as important or even necessary for success in life.

As with all things change-related, with new trends, it's of necessity for us to steadily explore, where the people who throw up these sentiments are coming from. As parents we should, because many of our children already believe these lines of thinking which also now impacts on their academics and our expectations of them.

In the past centuries, teachers were perceived as gods. They were so well educated and they were respected in society. There are many things that are not so certain about teachers of those times but it is in doubt that they were as supportive of children who were not as fast paced. They talked a lot about becoming excellent and they stood up for those standards.

As more research comes out, it is becoming increasingly obvious that children, to a large extent, deserve some sort of individual attention. There have been cases where children with great potential fell out and supportive teachers who noted them helped pull them through. I am a typical example.

There have been cases where children who teachers spoke negatively against, went on to succeed and so it has brought about different people undermining the teacher's value.

My second observation of the 21st century teacher is that for most of them, they did not set out to be teachers. Employment deficiencies took them that way and it's a tedious job to be in. This has resulted in a steady decline in the quality of instruction.

This and the fact that the government has stopped incentivizing the teaching profession and investing in education as a whole. If done otherwise, could have made teaching attractive to the people who found themselves in it and those who may be gifted to do it.

There have been teachers who became passionate about their students and eventually stayed on the job regardless of the poor working conditions. So, we have a mix of frustrated and passionate teachers in every setting. But isn't this the case in every profession?

Every time we say the quality of education is poor, the output of the poor education is our children. There have been children born with a lot of potential who get lost academically for one reason or the other. And as parents we judge far too quickly and allow shame determine our next line of action.

Many times, we take actions to save face and help our children far too quickly that it cripples the child in the same way helping a caterpillar out of the cocoon cripples the butterfly.

In this chapter, I want to address the shame that we feel as parents when our children are not doing well. This shame we feel is an unnecessary pressure and it does the child more harm than good.

Our children's failure does not need to make us feel as though we were failed parents. Even if our work schedules have contributed to the outcome, we can take a step back and make corrections and set the child going. Momentary failure need not be the reason our children are maimed for life.

What do I mean by maimed for life?

When a child does not do well in a particular subject or school, it is an injustice for us to look for ways to help the child to cheat the system. It is injustice for us to lobby for them to get a grade or an award for something they do not deserve.

We should praise our children at home and show them we love them but we must allow the systems designed to build them up function properly. Our children should be allowed to experience failure and learn from it. If we steadily protect them from it, when they show up at work and do tardy or lousy work and get penalized, what will they know to do?

How will they appreciate the standards which they should work towards if eventually we will have a way to work around it?

To succeed in the 21st century classroom our children and we as their parents must learn to do the following:

1.   We have to model a sense of responsibility towards school work. If as a parent, you continue to badmouth the school teacher or the school system as a whole, your child picks the cue to undervalue it and not take it seriously.

When children do not attribute value to a thing, they

will not give their best, they will not discover themselves like they ought to and regardless of the results or outcomes (brilliant children or not), they miss the most important thing that school was designed for, which is self-discovery.

2.   The second thing would be for our children to deal with the lies they pick up from school. The lies that certain subjects are easier than others or certain fields are for certain gender or that a teacher is picking on them. Is it possible for a teacher to pick on a child? Oh, yes! It is very, very possible. But children who learn to get the point of what the teacher is saying would do far better. It can be difficult to do this especially for teens but that's what they have parents for.

Parents are to help their children overcome prejudices so that they can truly learn. Parents are to also help their children with dialogues they have about their own capacities to do well. Yes, help them deal with the voices of self-doubt and presumption that they will be unsuccessful at certain task.

3. There are mundane things connected to academic success that many children do not know but should. These include tardiness, rough handwriting, going to bed late, overuse of technology, ever before we get to incomprehensible teachers.

4. We need to snap out of the luck mentality that believes that brilliant students are lucky or have something in their genes. Hard work and practice are prerequisites for success.

5.	This generation has an instant gratification problem. They get discouraged easily, quit easily, and do not work through things. Parents need to stand by their children and ensure they see through things. Let me share an example. I have my children stay in a particular school club for an entire school year ever before they consider changing.

It has helped me to teach my daughters that they do not drop what they have at the scent of excitement towards something or at a hint of difficulty. Today, they know that regardless of what they want, I will always be there to ensure they stay through to their initial commitment.

That child that loves arts and then suddenly moved when friends were moving to another club, as parents we must ask them to go back and sit through their commitment.

What has this got to do with grades? Everything! So, they love a subject until they get to the rigorous aspects. This is usually the place for marked growth and self-discovery. If they continue to dodge those parts and duck, at what point do they really mature?

So, tell your children and teens to ask questions in class. Ask them to calm down and look through processes carefully before they conclude that something is too difficult and not for them. Tenacity will help them succeed.

Parents need to be a pillar of support to their child in the 21st century. Getting a home lesson teacher is great especially because it gives a child that individual support. But reviewing their notes with them, discussing concepts from their books with them has a way of simplifying difficult concepts.

When you do explain like you do, you light them up to understand concepts that were taught in the past and many more that will be taught in the future.

6. The 21st century has brought with it the death of the siesta. Afternoon naps are gone. Some schools have students getting home at 6pm and some have homework and will sleep late and get up the next day.

Guess what? We are already running adult routines for them. This surely has an impact on their health at the end of the day. This can fog their sense of judgment and make them constantly irritable while misjudging their current realities.

<u>What should you do?</u>

1. **Have your children sleep better and for longer.**

In 2015, the National Sleep Foundation came up with an update on the recommended hours of sleep for persons of all ages;

- New-borns (0-3 months): Sleep range is 14-17 hours each day
- Infants (4-11 months): Sleep range is 12-15 hours
- Toddlers (1-2 years): Sleep range is 11-14 hours
- Pre-schoolers (3-5): Sleep range is 10-13 hours
- School age children (6-13): Sleep range is 9-11 hours.
- Teenagers (14-17): Sleep range is 8-10 hours
- Younger adults (18-25): Sleep range is 7-9 hours
- Adults (26-64): Sleep range is 7-9 hours
- Older adults (65+): Sleep range is 7-8 hours

"This is the first time that any professional organization has developed age-specific recommended sleep durations based on a rigorous, systematic review of the world scientific literature relating sleep duration to health, performance and safety," said Charles A. Czeisler, PhD, MD, chairman of the board of the National Sleep Foundation, chief of sleep and circadian disorders at Brigham and Women's Hospital, and Baldino Professor of Sleep Medicine at the Harvard

Medical School.

There is so much in this for everyone – parents, children and teens alike - to draw from.

2. Help your children to plan better.

Packing up bags and snacks the night before and other preparatory things like school uniforms, homework and all those kinds of things will go a long way in helping reduce the early morning tension. There is the other angle of getting someone to do the other things for them. We have to strike a balance. There should be chores done by them on say weekends and those they do for themselves to prepare them for the next day, so that they still do not miss out in taking personal responsibility of their welfare.

3. Manage the overwork effectively.

Overwork and stress also contributes to the panic that comes when they are faced with rigorous task at school

along with other problems such as with memory skills, attention, learning and behavior.

So, overwhelming school work plus use of devices is a recipe for disaster unless such a device was aiding school work. In which case, they should be effectively spaced out or not done often together.

4. Be a listening parent.

Regardless of your expectations, listen first. Share with your child about a time you were also under pressure and what you did to make a difference.

5. Teach problem-solving.

Seize the opportunity of the overwork to problem-solve with your child. Let them come up with several ways to work around the pressures and together pick the most suitable one to go with. However, always remind them that nothing is cast in stone. If an approach does not work as expected, then there is nothing wrong with trying another approach.

This should help them not get easily overwhelmed with any difficulty that comes while also building their resilience in the process.

What about when our children outrightly underperform?

Some children are underperforming because they are either learning with a learning style totally different from their preferred style.

Many do not have the discipline needed to manage the pressure at school, have parents not showing enough commitment to their school work, etc.

For many homes, parents are toxic and totally run them down because of failures at school. Many parents say this was how their own parents "drilled" them to work hard. Your 21st century child does not know as much as you knew back then about reality and being tenacious.

The blueprint of their success lies in helping them see that they can do well if they believe, plan, take steps and are consistent. And doing all of these from a place where they are convinced that they have their parent's support. Since our goal is to see them succeed let's create a path that leads towards success and not away from it.

Enforcing the standards or the pathway for success will not be a walk in the park and all, but it will not attack your child's sense of worth. If you and your child agree on steps to take, a violation should be met with an agreed consequence but not before the default has been put through a careful review that enables your child make an empowering decision when given another opportunity.

In other words, when they make mistakes, ask them to reflect and review lessons they have learned from the experience.

Step them up to take on rigorous school work but let them always know you are there to cheer them on.

I have written extensively on school behavior and success in my book, **"Back 2 School Success Kit"**

- Key Points

- School success in the 21st century will happen when children are allowed to go through the process without undue parental influence on the child's academic outcomes.
- Using verbally abusive words on a child who has failed is not nearly as empowering as holding them up to responsible school behavior standards and supporting them the whole way.
- Children whose parents show interest in their studies are most likely to place value on their educational process.

#6 THE RISE AND RISE OF ATTENTION SEEKING BEHAVIOURS

The 21st century is characterized by media tools such as the social media. These tools were designed to help us stay connected with friends and loved ones and share life's memories regardless of how far apart we are from each other physically.

Like with all things, there are now abuses of these platforms when they are seen to foster narcissistic tendencies – which are a deep need for excessive attention and admiration usually done to the extent of having no empathy for others.

There is a growing need to share pictures, videos or text about every aspect of one's life. Some persons take it to the point that it now appears as though they were living in their own reality TV set.

People are desperate to create an image online and sustain it, even if it means trampling on someone else. People shame others, blackmail others and display attention seeking behaviors online.

Many of our children are online posting, sharing and doing all sorts of things. At what point should we be concerned that the social media may be fostering narcissistic behaviors? At what point does an innocent post cross the line to be attention seeking behavior?

An attention seeking behavior entails acting in a way that is likely to elicit attention, usually to elicit validation from others. When a person who puts up a post online becomes extremely concerned with gaining attention or validation from what they post, then we have a bit of a problem on our hands.

When a young person (applies to anyone) is easily drawn to social media metrics like the number of followers, number of likes, shares and comments, etc. in a way that it is not about driving commerce or trade but rather from a place in which self-esteem is dependent on this metrics, then we can say convincingly that this is recipe for disaster.

This can be an emotionally exhausting place to be. Psychologists consider it a destructive addiction that is hurting our health.

Some platforms have explored these tendencies and indulged many of our children while cashing out massively. As parents, we have to step back and help them.

First, let's take some steps back and ask what the fuel for this behavior is. What makes a child crave attention? What does attention seeking on mediums such as social media look like?

I particularly love the way Marie Hartwell-Walker, puts it in her article, What To Do About Attention-Seeking Children. She says, straight to the point, that children who are attention-seeking have a legitimate need. And as parents, it's our job to teach them how to get it in a legitimate way.

This legitimate need could come from us not giving them enough uninterrupted attention. Often times, between going off on our minds and using our mobile phones, our children are left without the quality time and attention they need from us. The eye contact, the physical touch, etc. are gestures that help us communicate that our children have our attention.

"Parents who were themselves neglected, who are temperamentally more distant, or who are struggling with mental illness need to work to overcome their own issues for the sake of their children's psychological welfare.

Little children need to be cuddled, played with, talked to, read to, and tucked in at night to be emotionally secure and strong. Big children need their folks to share activities and meaningful conversations, to attend their events, and, yes, to give them hugs and pats on the back," says Marie Hartwell-Walker.

So, children would explore different means, even within our homes to draw attention.

According to nobullying.com these are the different types of attention seekers –

- Those that fake illness to get attention.

- The child that is overly dramatic.

- The child that causes harm to another person just to play the hero in the situation.

- The child that puts themselves as the leader in any situation to receive attention.

- The child that plays one parent against the other.

- The child that acts as though they are super busy

and over the top important so that it amazes people that they are able to complete everything on their plate.

- The one who pretends to be a victim over the smallest of situations.

It's important to seek to understand the root cause of their need for attention. Even simple scenarios where you unknowingly give one child attention over the other even for legitimate reasons as the child being in poor health can make the other act out.

There are also other underlying issues that lead to attention seeking behaviors such as trauma. Trauma can result from seemingly little things like changing environment to complex things like molestation or even the loss of a loved one.

While growing up, parents hardly ever paid attention to their children's emotional needs and reactions. Rather, many parents had the unrealistic expectation that regardless of the situation the children were in, they had to zip it up. Today's child would not zip it up. The truth is that no generation of children has ever been able to zip it up. None at all. Rather, they have grown older and thought that life was a certain way and drew conclusions for which they pour out the resentment on other people. In other words, we have recycled unresolved emotions, generation after generation. Let's make this the generation where hurts actually get resolved so that we can lead happier and more wholesome lives.

Social media just becomes a platform or window for our children to express their unresolved or resolved emotions. This can be easily seen in the way and manner they use social media and their motive for what they do on social media. Here is a bit of statistics on teens social media addiction;

- 92% of teens go online daily, and 24% say they go online "almost constantly."
- 76% of teens use social media (81% of older teens, 68% of teens ages 13 and 14).
- 71% of teens use Facebook, 52% use Instagram, 41% use Snapchat, 33% use Twitter, and 14% use Tumblr.
- 77% of parents say their teens get distracted by their devices and do not pay attention when they're together.
- 59% of parents say they feel their teen is addicted to their mobile device.

- 50% of teens say they feel addicted to their mobile device.

Sources: Pew Research Centre and Common-Sense Media

So how do we address all of these?

- Start from the roots. Affirm your child and also have them affirm themselves.
- Make out time for each child. Do not just say you love them, be there. Read with them. Spend time with them. Be available to each of them.
- When you see manipulative, attention seeking behavior, pull them away and ask them to use words. Always encourage them to say what they mean and mean what they say.
- Walk them through their thoughts so that you shine light on other perspectives and possibilities. Through this you can help them identify wrong, faulty thinking. This means you will listen.
- Give them the time to get over their emotions.
- Please stick with the family standards, do not sway. Be firm and be fair.
- Steadily reinforce family traditions that make everyone feel loved.
- Walk your children through authority attribution. Essentially, this means, processing what makes them believe a random like on their post or shares brings a sense of worth.
- Help them see social media audiences for who they are, typical strangers who do not know them enough for their perspective about them to count.

- Key Points

- When you have a child that excessively wants to be liked, then it is an indication of a problem that should be addresses.
- Children who are attention seeking have a legitimate need. As parents, our responsibility is to teach them how to meet the need in a legitimate way.
- Young children need hugs and cuddles. Older children need companionship, hugs, and pats on the back.
- As parents, we should pay attention to all the cues that show your child needs attention and may be starved of affection, regardless of their age.

#7 THE NEW NARRATIVE ON LOVE, SEX, MARRIAGE & EVERYTHING IN BETWEEN

While growing up as children, we had our own narratives on what love looked like. For our grandparents, they would meet the person they were going to spend their lives with on the day of their marriage and it seemed to work.

It seemed to work back then because people were content and it wasn't really within the realm of possibility, at least in thought, that it could be done otherwise.

Our generation focused a lot on true love. Someone sort of like a soul mate - made for you. People will begin a relationship and take an oath and all sorts.

Today's children are waking up in the face of failed case studies of true love. They have seen their own parents, parents of their friends and neighbors just walk away.

There is a quest for getting what is workable.

So, this generation is essentially experimenting. They say the heart wants what it wants. This calls for concern.

Sex was supposed to be held in high esteem but their generation is swamped with tales and experiences of child molestation, sexual abuse, infidelity and all sorts of sex for cash experiences. So, this totally throws away the validity of some of our claims to them.

Unfortunately, our claims are valid, just because a few people, in moments of selfishness and sometimes confusion, threw away caution, we eventually ended up modeling a totally different vibe than we intended.

It's chaotic out there for them. This generation has so much sexually themed entertainment and this is inducing a lot of risky behaviors and it's rather unfortunate, they do not see enough adults upholding a totally different standard.

There are not enough parents who even know that their children are addicted to porn and it's unfortunate that some of them find porn on the phones of their parents and even surf the web for porn from the phones of their parents. So many of us parents are distracted.

Lust and the pull towards sex are very strong. It is always best to talk wholesomely with children and open up early enough in age appropriate ways. Yes, emphasis is age appropriate and while doing this, do not expose them or allow them to expose themselves to sex, seduction lingo and contents on TV or online.

Usually, I like parents to know that, their children's body works in about the same way the adult body works if not more. If they watch a certain clip no matter how short, it leaves ideas and imagery behind that pulls their curiosity in and draws them to experimentation. So, teach the rules and really how the mind works around this thing beyond just giving instructions.

First and foremost, sex education conversations are not as intimidating as we make it. When it feels intimidating, you are definitely going to misfire. Yes, you are going to either say too much or too little.

Sex education at all times needs to be age-appropriate.

The conversation with children at age 1 - 5 and possibly 7 should cover information about private and public body parts. There are tons of music videos that you can download and start out on this topic. Tell them what good touch and bad touch is.

Also, tell them about the people who make up their safe circle. Their safe circle is made up of the persons they should run to or talk to when they feel uncomfortable. You give them the list of persons that are trusted to be in this circle.

It is always important to ask them to never follow people to a secluded place alone. Be it a teacher, cousin, uncle or a friend.

At this age, when children ask where children come from, it really is out of sheer curiosity and not a sexual question. You could explain the process to them by saying that children are born through the vagina.

You can also add that the body is incredible, and makes some adjustment which makes it possible for the baby to come out through that part of the body. You could also mention that babies are usually a lot smaller than when they are born.

If there has been a caesarean birth in your family, then you are twice lucky because you would say your tummy was cut open but usually you will still need to talk about the other way.

I have heard people say that children are increasingly sexualized these days making the age for full blown Sex Ed (sex education) to be lowered. But I do not believe that all of a sudden, we need to go around believing that all children know about sex.

Maybe we should ask how children of younger ages, got access to content that exposed them to sex, be it through videos or verbal conversations or even physical touch and even bumping into parents caught right in the act. When we find out where the access is, we can plug the holes.

As precautionary measures, parents need to lock their doors while having sex, watch what their children are exposed to online and on TV, and stop making excuses about what shows they see in the presence of their children.

A child's life is never the same after they are exposed to sexual content. It alters lives and distracts them in ways unimaginable.

The second level is the 7 - 10. Sex education at this age should be about pre- puberty education, where we begin to talk about some of the bodily changes they should expect and hygiene very importantly.

The school curriculum does not talk about sexual intercourse until in JSS 1 when they are learning reproductive system in the manner of penis and vagina as reproductive parts and even in those times and situations, procreation is the theme not the pleasure. It is still sex education even when you do not talk about orgasm. I recommend that you speak with your child before anyone else does.

Any form of education that guides a child on what is happening in their bodies and what is the right use or abuse of their sexual parts is in place.

Pre-puberty, especially on the late stages, can be a good time to talk about sex in terms of how the menstruation system works. Sex education is a lot easier when you have rapport with your children enough for them to ask you candid questions and for them to even bring up conversations whenever they arise.

Beyond what we say to them or expect to be sex education, there will be rumors and myths flying around per time. It is important for them to be able to come to you for guidance per time.

By the time you have preteens and teens, sex education must go side by side with self-esteem because during those ages sex is sought for as a tool for gaining validation. That is, the idea that they are beautiful if a boy or girl asks them out and gives them their own body or such is interested in their (your child's) own body.

Again remember that sex education is not about how to have sex; rather, it is about how not to abuse your sexual parts.

Essentially sex education always needs to be age appropriate and contextual. If a child is raped at a young age, Sex Ed will be different. It will have to incorporate esteem building, what is right and wrong, and how they can place a higher value on themselves beyond how they feel in their bodies. Rape incidents should not be hidden. The child should be taken to the hospital and provision should be made to speak with a therapist.

Priority should be placed on helping the child overcome the blame and shame that the child may feel. Parents should also believe older children who come home to say they were raped.

Some teens and even young women are raped and during the experience, they reach an orgasm. Does that make them bad people or irresponsible? No! Our body is a system. We can be responsive to certain stimuli. Explaining concepts such as this is also a part of education.

Should you talk with your teens about condoms and contraceptives? Yes, you should.

While it's important to protect them from occurrences of sexually transmitted diseases and unplanned pregnancy with the possibility of abortions that could expose them to unnecessary risk, it is also important to teach them about self-restraint and removing themselves from tempting situations.

Yes, condoms and contraceptives may well protect them from sexually transmitted diseases (STDs) and unplanned pregnancies but that is not all that there is about sex. It is important to mention, that after sexual exposures, girls were more than twice as likely as boys to say they felt bad about themselves. Girls were also more than three times as likely to say they felt used as a result of having sex. Meaning that, having sex can ruin a girl's self-esteem afterwards.

Those findings may partly stem from society's double standard about sex. We would do a better service to their generation if we police our boys just as much as girls. The double standard makes the credibility of the said standard fluid.

I did some research a few days ago about what the consequences for sex was other than pregnancy and Sexually Transmitted Diseases. And I found that everything we have ever listed was either directly connected to or was a by-product of STDs and unplanned pregnancy. So, now that we are telling them about condoms and contraceptives those two appear to take care of our fears. It seems as though we have nothing else to say.

With the education on condoms and contraceptives, teens can, most of the time, believe that they will be fine.

Yes, we have to remind them that sometimes they will forget to use condoms but what if they assure us, they would not. By the way, there are no guarantees that they would not.

What else is strong enough to consider as a possible consequence for premarital sex?

Yes, God doesn't want us having premarital sex. The teens know but they still go on to have sex. So maybe telling them why God doesn't want that to the best of what we know may be helpful.

Paul Bois puts it aptly, "God's call to chastity is about liberating people from being slaves to their passions."

They need to know that many times urges to have sex are from the wrong motivations. Such as using sex as a means of validation of gaining control, and because the motive is wrong, they will most likely hurt themselves and hurt others. They will abuse their own body and mind.

They will lead lives of false hopes, wrong expectations, disappointment and desperation. They will recycle baggage after baggage.

With all things about wrong motivation, it will drive us to do things and we will lose control, act out poor judgment, get ourselves into avoidable trouble and will lose our sense of direction in the process.

The most dangerous thing to live by is to want what your body wants. Your flesh (body) always wants what is not right for you. Let's think about cravings for the very food that may be unhealthy for you.

Wrong motivations are insatiable. They can only be addressed. Because of the insatiable nature of wrong motivations, from sex, people will go into other vices. So once a standard has been defied, it becomes a slippery slope towards other vices.

There are schools of thoughts that young people subscribe to that tell them they own their own bodies and can do whatever they want. On the face value, it appears as though it's an empowering perspective but I tend to believe it opens another door where people become slaves of their own lust. Either ways, no one should live by clichés like "the heart wants what it wants" or "you can't help who you love".

Each one of these lines takes away the power of objectivity from young people.

There are probably a lot more consequences that have far reaching impact on our lives beyond unplanned pregnancies and STDs. There is life after the euphoria.

There is life beyond orgasms. Young boys and girls need to know this and know it early enough. Having fair, square, straight conversations about sex is important.

Here is a simple guide to age appropriate sex education:

<u>Six things you need to know about sex education.</u>

1. Sex education conversations are not as intimidating as we make it. When it feels intimidating, you are definitely going to misfire. Yes, you are going to either say too much or too little.
2. Sex education at all times needs to be age-appropriate and delivered in layers.
3. Writing out the outline of what you want to say is very important.
4. Hold this conversation when the atmosphere is right, Right here implies that your children are really free with you enough to open up to you.
5. The best sex education is not just about what you say but creating an atmosphere where your child can always come to you when they have a question or need clarification even long after you have had the talk.
6. There are different types of sex education; age-

based sex education, observation-led sex education and need-based sex education.

Age-based sex education is what you say to your children at different ages. They are things that your children should know at a certain age. For example, from the time children are 2, they should learn about 'no-no' body parts.

Observation-led sex education is what you have to say because of what you have observed. For example, if your children are beginning to watch a lot of romantic movies, or you notice they have a love interest or are beginning to act suspicious, there are things you have to teach regardless of their age.

Need-based sex education is what you have to teach because a need has arisen. For example, a child who was raped or had a friend who was raped, does not need silence. They have to learn about sex, consent and protecting themselves

Principles for giving sex education

Hygiene. First things first. For parents having difficulty opening sex education conversations, hygiene gives a simple entry point that makes a big difference.

Layer by layer approach. Even in school, you learn

gradually. Do not be in a hurry to teach everything. Ensured that children completely understand what you have taught before going to the next layer. Give some time before going to another later.

Ask questions. Make it a typical learning module. Make it fun but make sure you ask questions. It is not effective if you are the only one doing the talking. Ask questions but do not ask questions that make them uncomfortable and avoid being confrontational too.

Try a Do-It-Yourself approach. When necessary, bring action to the learning experience. Let them do something in the process.

Keep the communication lines open. Leave room for further talk. Let the child know that they can always come back for further talk.

Light Introduction of Subsequent Layers. Prep for the next layer. If you drew an outline then you know where you would be going to next. If you do, throw in a little bit of the next layer.

Guide to giving age appropriate sex education | Age 0 – 2

- Names and functions of body parts.

- If they have a sibling of the opposite gender, teach them difference in boys and girls.

- The places to be naked and the places not to be.

- 'No no' body parts. (next layer)

- Quick tip: use nursery rhymes

- Talk about faith-based standards and principles. (our body should be honored and so should other people's bodies be)

Guide to giving age appropriate sex education | Age 2 – 5

- Private and public parts (good touch and bad touch.

- What to do when someone tries to touch your private parts.

- Having a safe circle: people to talk to when you feel uncomfortable with someone.

- Exceptions to good touch, bad touch (E.g. when doctors and nurses have to care, plus boundaries to their own touch)

- They too should not touch someone else in their private area. (next layer)

- Quick tip: write the names of people in their safe circle and why you chose them.

- Talk about faith-based standards and principles.

Guide to giving age appropriate sex education | Age 5 – 7

- Consent. Don't hug or touch someone if they don't want to be touched. Always ask if you can.

- No secrets about good touch or bad touch.

- How to say no if someone wants to touch you.

- Physical boundaries: E.g. Don't follow someone to anywhere where there is no one. Don't take gifts from someone and in exchange follow them.

- Mental boundaries: If someone said you should do something wrong if not, they report you, let them know that its okay for your parents to know. If someone says they would hurt your parents, if you talked, you can be quiet but always know they cannot. Reinforce that you will believe them.

- Talk about faith-based standards and principles.

Guide to giving age appropriate sex education | Age 8 -10

- Reinforce physical and mental boundaries.

- Learn about puberty; Physical changes in the body.

- Learn about puberty; Hygiene

- Learn about puberty; Periods and wet dreams.

- Learn about internal reproductive system (But not necessarily intercourse)

- Talk about faith-based standards and principles.

Guide to giving age appropriate sex education | Age 10 -12

- Crushes: what to do about intense emotions and when you have a strong liking for someone.

- Love Vs Infatuation

- Redefining friendships

- Sex: Vagina, Penis. How it happens, what can happen afterwards and when it is the right time to have sex. (Choices and Consequences)

- Talk about faith-based standards and principles.

Guide to giving age appropriate sex education | Age 12 – 14

- Sex: Why there are urges for sex. What to do about urges. (responsibilities, choices and consequences)

- Sexually Transmitted Infections (STIs) and Sexually Transmitted Diseases (STDs)

- Condoms and Contraceptives

- Family rules for sex and dating (Conversational yet firm)

- Address Myths and What Ifs

- Use a lot of TV story scenarios and situations to drive conversations.

- Talk about faith-based standards and principles.

Guide to giving age appropriate sex education | Age 14 - 18

- Self-love and the search for validation

- Defining relationships and timing

- Personal goals

- Reinforce everything between age 8 and age 14.

- Talk about faith-based standards and principles.

- Key Points

- Sex education has to be age appropriate.
- Parents must model high standards on sexual relationships.
- Yes, we should teach about condoms and contraceptives.
- We should help our children see that concepts such as 'the heart wants what it wants' are dangerous because, your body usually craves what is not good for you. A typical example will be how the body craves sugar even though it is dangerous for our health.

#8 THE WOKE GENERATION

Oh yes, this is the 'woke' generation. This is the movement generation.

To be woke means to be alert to injustice in society.

This generation is again on the quest to challenge everything it has been taught. They see inconsistencies, they see partiality, they see insensitivity and it turns everything they have been told upside down.

At the beginning of this book, I talked about how innovation and change are borne out of our needs and challenges and how we try to address issues.

I am a mother of two daughters and when it was time to start giving them responsibilities at home, in terms of chores, I noticed that I was going to tow the path way that I was raised. The path way where the woman is overworked and always grinding and then loses herself in service to others, while her male contemporary is taught to expect to be served of others.

So, I decided to teach them about asking for help, sharing tasks and taking a break when they need a break, you can ask for it. While teaching how to wash plates, I am also teaching about hacks that make it easy. I am asking the older to co-wash with me.

These kinds of adjustments are necessary today as we have seen many fear-based rules fall like a pack of cards in all our faces. For example, telling girls to learn housekeeping so that "they can be married" is an injustice to a generation. Everyone should learn housekeeping so that as they go ahead and marry (if they want to) they come in as partners and not as a master waiting to be served and a slave expected to slave herself away.

I need for us to know that this generation is responding from the failures of past generation.

Many young people today are hurting from abuse by the very authority figures that were to take care of them. They have seen failures of parents, spiritual and school leaders. Lecturers have had students sleeping with them and guess what, this generation have little or no regards for authority.

You would often hear them taunt with slogans such as "who e epp" (who did it help). This generation is hurting from the failure of their support systems from parents, to spiritual leaders and those in government. Their plea is legitimate, even though their approach may not yield the impact they need.

They do, however, need to redirect their energies. In the meantime, they are the biggest influencers of your children. They control the social media and our children believe they are absolutely right.

So, it means you have to help your children articulate how to direct their energies to strategically addressing the challenges they hurt about;

This generation is fighting just about anything. Here are some of their fights and what they can do about it:

Governance

They want to know how we are governed. What gives one person the legitimacy to rule over the rest of us? This consciousness is coming out of dissatisfaction with the output of governance.

So, they come on social media and from the place of this dissatisfaction they vent, they meme, they scorn, and they disrespect.

This may be not a good place to start. But you have to be ready to teach them about taking personal responsibility as well and being civil while performing their civic duties.

Do not shut down their need to know. Teach them constructive criticism, so that they do not become tools.

As parents, we should not be indifferent about governance and we should not propagate falsehood.

We need to be very careful about labeling people by religion and tribe. Our children will not tolerate it and they will turn on us. The woke generation is working very hard to be color blind, religion blind and ethnicity blind.

Staying objective helps. And if your children become gullible to the prejudices of ethnicity and religion, then we have a dangerous generation to contend with.

Always have it in mind that, sooner or later, they will ask you what you did to make this country better. The truth is that if we shape them right, they have the capacity to pursue our collective good.

Gender Based Violence

Whether it is a man abusing a woman or a woman abusing a man, this generation will not suffer in silence.

This generation is not buying the approaches we have previously used in addressing this issue.

Neither are they buying into the idea that women should just sit down and pray for abusive, cheating men. They will not in the name of being 'strong men' sit there and 'be a man' 'in the face of violent women as spouses.

There are statistics to show for avoidable deaths arising from domestic violence. It is also unfair for family members to insist on saving face at the expense of their child's life.

It calls for us adults to review what we have always held on to and lived by along with the consequences that we have suffered. This generation wants wholesome experiences where people are not dying slowly or suddenly in the hands of violent spouses.

Dear parent, this generation also wants parents to listen when they are concerned about a person, they may like but their parents would not. They want parents to hear them out. They also want their parents to fight off friends that want to bring them down. Yes, they know the friend is a bad influence.

They argue about it in front of you but they do not want you to stop looking out for them. Maybe it is because in many ways, they are trying to severe the friendship but do not know exactly what to do.

They also do not want to see their parents fight. Have issues but do not fight. They carry the fears of what may happen one day. Many of them find escape from these kinds of pressures in drugs, casual sex and everything in between.

As parents, it is our responsibility to pursue wholesome, well- thought through views on issues. I would not tell my girls that a violent husband can change, I would not. But I will tell my son, if he finds that he has violent tendencies, just like I would tell my daughter if she had violent tendencies that they need to get help.

As a Christian, I will recommend a Christian therapist and I will also let them know that violent tendencies come from personal unresolved issues and have nothing to do with what another person did or not.

The need for therapy

This generation is open to seeking professional help. As a parent, I would push for personal responsibility side by side with professional help. It is important to note that therapists do not whisk away issues. They take people on a journey to make their own adjustments.

Essentially, let's not make therapist the new escape, just as we did to our spiritual affiliations. As a Christian, there is so much direction about what to do next.

Many times, we want a quick snap and when it does not happen, we ascribe failure to the person or to the system.

Disability

Africa has been characterized by subsistence thinking. This was a situation where everyone just looked out for their own best interest. And so, if you didn't have a child with disability, it was completely alien to you what their reality was like. It was convenient to make up stories as the cause of one disability or the other.

I recall while growing up that there were people, I came in contact with at school that were different and even in the family circle. Today, I know better how to relate with them and there are a lot more resources available on how to teach them and support them so that they can make the best out of their lives.

The woke generation wants more empathy and thankfully on January 23rd, 2019, Discrimination against Persons with Disabilities (Prohibition) Act which would see corporate entities and individuals face excruciating sanctions if found guilty of discriminating against persons with impairments, was signed into law by President Muhammadu Buhari of Nigeria.

As parents, we need to strive to be informed about issues and not be too quick to judge other parents of children who are different.

Some disabilities are more obvious than others and sometimes children that appear to be unruly in public places could be living with a disability.

Feminism

This generation has the voices of Chimamanda Adichie and other young people; male and female, who are fiercely for or against feminist principles. Some of their views seem extreme but we should not throw away the baby with the bath water. This generation, unlike others is not going to sit on the fence. It's all a scream for empathy.

More empathy when a woman loses her spouse, more empathy for women at the workplace, more empathy for women who are in relationships and those who have been in failed relationships.

And after empathy, let us show respect. A woman is a full-blown human being and should be accorded with the same respect that would be accorded to a man. A woman should be seen for what contributions she can make and not side-lined, or under-rewarded just because she is a woman. Yes, everyone should be given opportunity to lead if they have the capacity to do so.

These concerns are first about 'women' and then when you look a little bit more deeply, you realize that 'women' also means your 'sister', your 'daughter', your 'mum.

It's time to let some of the cultural practices that hold us back go. It is time to break stereotypes and see ourselves as human beings first. That's what our children want and that's what a greater percentage of their generation believe is right and I am happy to say, it is time to look at our common humanity. Any culture that makes us insensitive to each other should be frowned at regardless of our gender.

Faltering models

This generation is snapping out of the culture of pretense where even though our parents felt a certain way about a person, whenever the person visited, they pretended otherwise. There is also the problem of parents whose lives are marred by all kinds of failures yet trying to enforce standards. This is leading to rebellion at dimensions that have never been seen or experienced. And that is the problem with rebellion, it just sets off uncontrollably. They conclude on people and situations too quickly.

Parents have to strive to be role models this time

around.

Fashion

The rebellion is seen in aspects such as fashion. The dialogues are on. For example, why should a man rape a woman because of what she wore? What if what I am wearing makes me more comfortable? The social media and movies tell a tale of fashion in other climes and right over here, our young people feel like why not?

There are ongoing debates about different things; whether people should be judged by what they wear. Conversations around decency are challenged headlong until a young person needs a job application.

Yes, we will continue to demand that men should be brought to justice in situations of rape. There are no grounds, in my opinion of connecting what a person wears to an action that someone can control himself around. She can wear crazy and you have a choice to either ask her for consensual sex or walk away altogether.

In the same breathe, we will continue to talk about decency, keeping private parts private and dressing in the ways we want to be addressed. As a parent, I am careful about describing what my daughters wear as 'hot" or what I wear as 'sexy 'because it means to me that, I am dressing for sex appeal.

So, the other day, my daughter asked 'do not I look hot?', and I said 'you look amazing'. In that way, we meet their quest to counter culture with a sense of responsibility and not revolt.

In the face of all of this uproar, today's child needs a mentor. And the safest place and easiest and most readily available person to serve as their mentor should be their parent.

The need for mentors

To mentor this generation, you have to acquire knowledge and be informed. You cannot bully or scold them out of rebellion. They would, at most, keep calm in your presence but go on to lead a totally different life.

It's in mentoring that you can, for instance, talk to your child who does not trust politicians to use his app building skills to develop an app or build a website that does some listing for politicians past antecedents or even run a media outlet that interviews politicians and just has a backlog of several interviews that can become a reference material.

Through mentoring, we can direct their energy towards productive living.

- **Key Points**

- Think of this generation as the one screaming at the failures of the past generations.
- As parents we need to rethink some of the things we have accepted as culture and passed down one generation after another.
- We also need to strive to expand our knowledge base to understand things that are alien to us before we label them.
- This generation needs parents who would serve both as role models and as mentors.

#9 THE 21ST CENTURY FAMILY STRUCTURE.

The 21st century has a totally different family setting than what was obtainable in times past. The difference can be seen primarily in the structure and composition of today's families.

Structure

Most families back then were a bit straight forward; nuclear in every sense of the word. There was a father, a mother and children living together but then they also had lots and lots of relatives who lived with them. Today's family structure is a bit different. We have the regular - mother, father and children but we also have other family structures;

The blended families

This is a family structure made up of a father and mother along with their step children and own children.

In this arrangement, there are usually at least four clusters of people who have a voice in these kinds of family.

In a situation where the woman had children before she got married to the man, there is an implication that her immediate family and her children's fathers' family also have a voice in their family decisions.

This applies to the man as well.

Single parents
This is a second family structure that is common in the 21st century. There are many single parents who currently live alone and cater for their child or children. Both women and men currently serve as single parents even though the most predominant situation is with mothers being single parents.

The situations are different for each of the single parent family. Some are as a result of a personal decision to not marry the man or woman with whom they have a child and some have arisen from separation.

I will like to take out the situations where the single parent did not marry the father or mother of their child. This situation can be an interesting one if the one partner who is not with the child remarries. It can be a source of mistreatment and misunderstandings from both ends.

Usually, I just love to remind us that there is already so much pain, there are children involved and there is no need to create more pains for ourselves and the children.

There are also single parents who have deadbeat or run-away partners. A deadbeat partner refuses to show up in the life of the child like he or she should.

This can usually be a source of low esteem and recipe for behavior issues as these children begin to look for a means to draw the attention, they believe they are starved of. Unfortunately, they would usually act out on the one partner who is available to them.

The run-away never shows up. Never ever shows up. I remember vividly well the first book I started writing in 2009 and really never got around to finishing it. It held a lot of emotions for me. Looking back, it may have been therapeutic for me to just write.

I had just gotten married at 25 the previous year and started a family of my own, and to my own continual disappointment, my biological father never came for me. We had never sat across each other in a room to talk. I had never received a phone call and it was him.

There were times that it broke me at the core and made me so desperate for validation. Then I began to heal. He still has not come but as I got older, I scrutinized my own motives for wanting him to come. I looked my personal insecurities in the face.

Gradually, I healed. I have learnt to see my life from a much more holistic lens than one that just narrows into one aspect of my life.

Children for which one parent never shows up carry a badge of rejection with them. They need the right support system but not people that indulge them.

My husband once told me, "Someone cannot reject what he has not experienced." So, I realized that not showing up and rejection can be two different things. And even in the face of rejection, I should at the barest minimum accept and be kind to myself.

Can you see that long paragraph I just finished now? That is the kind of dialogue that dominates the lives of children in single parent families. Unfortunately, many never live through to heal.

Please if you get a woman pregnant or give birth to a child, note that you do not need to be with the father or mother of the child.

However, it is your primary responsibility to show up for the child.

If you perceive that their father/mother may be toxic, write letters, send pictures, be financially responsible for them, do whatever it takes to make your child see through to your personal effort regardless if the pregnancy was unplanned.

Let me also leave a caveat here. Being a child who was rejected by a parent is not a guarantee that you would succeed. Nature does not respond to self-pity. Yu can be rejected and fail woefully in life. The later has nothing to do with the former. Just like everyone else, you have to set goals and focus on what really counts. Be deliberate to make choices that lead you towards your goals.

I found that about everyone on earth has something they are hurting from or used to hurt from. For some, it's the hurt of abuse, loss of parents, sudden hardships etc. Being rejected by a parent is one of human's inhumanity to man. The good news is that, while we may not be able to control the reality surrounding our birth, we can choose our way to a desirable future.

Now that's powerful.

Divorce

Then finally, let's talk about growing rates of divorces and separation. The 21st century surely has relatively higher numbers of families dealing with divorce situations. Children are caught between. They now shuttle two homes during holidays and weekends and sometimes have to do this right in the middle of court hearings and divorce proceedings.

Children continue to love their parents but sometimes must pretend otherwise so that the other partner does not hurt.
This is a bit more complicated than I can find the words to articulate.

When divorce or separation happens, the children hurt deeply. Parents must know this.

Composition

The 21st century family also differs in composition. Prior to today, family clusters comprised primarily of members of one's immediate family and relatives.

Even people who served as helps most likely had a biological connection to the family. It was not uncommon to find younger siblings going along with older ones when they got married so that they could help tend to their nieces and nephews.

Today's society has so quickly changed and become so fast paced that younger ones who are not so young at the time of marriage of the older ones, are also planning their lives. It's not uncommon to hear parents say, "my child cannot go and be anyone's slave." This has yet given rise to a new set of realities, some of which are captured below.

Foster families

These are families that in addition to their own children have other children who may or may not be their relatives living under their care.

Many times, these families have a seamless life but there are situations where the children whom they have brought in to cater for, continually feel overwhelmed with resentment because their ideal form of family should be with their biological parents.

These families can have a longer journey on correcting and grooming and even showing love to the foster children across board.

For the purpose of all my writings, foster children are children you raise in your home who are not your biological children.

Culturally mixed families

There is a relatively higher number of mixed families in the 21st Century than in the previous generations. Today's families are multi-ethnic and truly this speaks volumes about the growth in our national integration. Many husbands today come from tribes different from those of their wives and may not even speak the same language as their partners. Thus breaking the often tightly held belief that language may be a force for unity.

While this statement may hold true, today's generation embraces that people are who they are regardless of where they come from. This has further helped us to be more accepting and has also reduced the problem of stereotyping by ethnicity.

Howbeit, this reality is also eroding our tribal languages and presents an opportunity for yet another innovation that should help African families, though multi-ethnic, to still pass on such legacies as language and precious cultures.

Yes, we have beautiful cultures that do not abuse anybody's rights and this should be upheld.

What can today's parents do, considering our current realities and the fast-changing possibilities of our emerging future?

Acceptance of the existing family structures:
Parents need to overcome their need to point fingers at the peculiarity of today's family's structures.

They are what they are but more so they are a product of the actions and inactions of previous generations. Many of the heartbreaks that today's families have had to live with come from the shortcomings of the previous families.

These shortcomings include not modeling the right values, not teaching and even to creating stereotypes that were detrimental to their children. Many families of old had parents who were selfish and ended up raising children who were entitled. We, therefore, need to demonstrate empathy for our peers who are raising children in unique circumstances and ensure that our children do not ask them or their children at school funny questions.

For starters, you, do not ask why their surnames are different.

While having our little conversations at home, we need to do away with some words like "illegitimate children."

No child under the sun is illegitimate or a bastard, even if the process of their coming to the world may have happened outside the four walls of the marriage institution.

Thus, we should avoid putting labels on these children.

Show empathy to families living these realities
We have to show empathy and understanding. Reach out to the children and show them love.

Sometimes, their perspective of life may be very discouraging, so they need to see people who go all out to show them love, just so that they can see another side of life.

Yes, relate, love and show care for children of single parents, children of divorced parents. They need it.

Help the children within these families see that they can remold.

This is the part I love the most. Yes, putting power back into the hands of a person to remold. I was raised by a single mum with the magnanimous support of her parents (my grandparents) and her siblings.

Right in that home, I told myself that even though my uncles were really awesome - Oh, yes! Kudos to every one of them - I still believed the ideal was for me to get married and for my husband and I to raise our children together. My uncles went through a lot of inconveniences for me and I do appreciate that but I sincerely didn't want to do it the way I saw it.

If you are a single parent or dealing with some unique experience in your family, please do not give that experience the power to shape the future of your children.

Love may have appeared to hurt you, but still give your children the belief that it will be different for them". Prepare them to be great partners and teach them how to identify great partners.

Please do not prepare them for failure. Do not prepare them with the motive that things will repeat. Bring hope. Trust again. If not for yourself, try trusting for your children.

Every generation has the ability and power to create a new set of realities. If we can do this for technology and tweak technology to serve us, then we have at least 18 years to raise human beings with a new crop of ideals. People who will uphold fairness, empathy and a have strong sense of responsibility.

In doing so, we would have created harmony in the world today and for generations to come.

Do not try to be their messiah

Be there for them, but do not try to be a messiah. Many of these families are healed already. Yes, there are indeed those hurting.

While some of these family structures may not appear to be our ideal, we need to realize that the current frame and form may compensate.

Some blended families are reminders of tempestuous journeys and how life pieced them together to heal and grow. In many ways, it compensates for the pain.

Some divorces, have paved a way for people to redefine themselves and see clearly their own value. Some people have learned from mistakes and have gone ahead to build lives more intentionally and with a lot more empathy. Sadly, though, there are dysfunctional families that look like the ideal family structure but aren't in reality.

Prepare your children to be with people who have children and drop the stigma

Extended families are usually the biggest source of pressure to relatives who get into relationships with people who have already had children.
Too many lies are told. If he has a son, they may be of the opinion that everything he is working for will go to that son and a 'strange woman'. Some have cases to show but many times they are either hearsays or the outcome of family manipulations.

Expect that you will raise children who can stand on their own with or without inheritances. Let your partner know clearly that as you both build together; every child of that family would have a fair share.

As much as possible, investment should also be made towards the child who is outside of the new family's immediate structure.

Let us kill the step-mother, step-father syndrome in this generation. Let us be only mother and father. Let's show empathy and deal with our need to manipulate realities.

- **Key Points**

- Family structures today are a reflection of the actions and inactions of previous generations.
- Family structures are different. Avoid asking siblings why they have different surnames.
- There is no such thing as a 'bastard' or an 'illegitimate child'. Every human being regardless of how they came to this world is equal in dignity.
- It is absolutely okay to marry someone who was raised by a single parent, someone who has been divorced or someone who has children. People's character should be the focus when making marriage decisions.

#10 HELPING YOUR CHILDREN FIND THEIR FEET IN THE WORLD

So many parents worry about their children falling behind in life, not marrying the right person or choosing/finding the right kind of work. We have concerns that in the overflowing recognition of talents, purpose and all of the shenanigans, that our children may actually be misled.

The real question is "how do we raise children in preparation for a future we do not know exactly what it would look like?" I mean, let us be honest.

Many parents believe that they have it all figured out. Read this course, go abroad for masters and then boom, marry there and stay back! Work spaces all over the world are changing fast and keeping pace or innovating altogether is the key.

Take a look at the 21st century employment structure today; there are full time workers who work for government or corporate organization as well as entrepreneurs.

Entrepreneurship is a broad term for all kinds of human innovation. People are making careers out of just about anything.

The array of careers includes those that are creating innovations, devices, experiences that move us towards ease, affordability and convenience.

Unlike how gloomy employment rates are painted, this is the best time to be born in terms of having a wider range of choices of what one can do. Why do I say so and how can you take advantage of it as a parent?

1.   **The 21st century has opened up individuals to labour markets beyond where they are**, beyond the borders of where they were born or what kind of education they might have had. Success today is determined by knowledge, skills, grit and raw determination.

Today's companies advertise jobs and get employment request from people across the globe that have the requisite skills for the job.

2. **There is availability of knowledge in ways that have never been.** There are now opportunities to take courses offered by the best universities across the globe, all from your mobile device. Quite interestingly, if you are looking for knowledge in a field that may not have been fully developed, you can still find short courses and free videos online.

3. **Today's workplace requires resourcefulness.** Resourcefulness - the ability to find quick and clever ways to overcome difficulties. This is the problem-solving generation. You can build it into your children from a very young age and they would be ready to go.

It is also important to note, that many of your children may have inbuilt resourcefulness that can be latent and go untapped when you do not pay attention.

How can you foster this important skill in your home?
• Ask your children for input when making key decisions. Ask questions on how best to use little to do much. Ask questions like how do we use the remaining bottles of water to make tea, boil rice, etc.?

• When drawing up family plans, have them make inputs in consideration of all the parameters possible. By teaching them decision-making skills, we raise resourceful individuals all squared up for success.

• Give them chores. Planning around chores can be a huge opportunity to foster resourcefulness.

• Turn moments of their misbehavior to skill building time. Yes, turn them to teachable moments.

The other day, I got home and needed to use the glue. On asking for it, I got to know that number 2 had spilled it and there was none left.

Honestly, there was no need to raise my voice because it would not bring back the glue.

What I did instead was to call her and tell her that I needed to use glue and she needed to advise me on the alternative to use. She thought for a while and then said, "Mummy, I think you should use cello tape."

•	Get your children thinking.

•	Do not be quick to dole out advice or answers. When your children are experiencing difficulties, brainstorm with them. Let them come up with different solutions and choose the ones that most adequately solve the problem.

Encourage hands-on activities like arts, crafts, recycling, building, etc. Make it a priority to invest periodically in this.

Other reasons the 21st century is the best time to be born in include;

4.	**The market is open and welcoming to unconventional useful solutions - innovations.** There was a time the business world was generally satisfied with people only offering quality services to their customers. That was until we met disruptors - people who look at existing systems and create solutions that either save time, money or bring about convenience and in many cases offer all three.

New business models have arisen and succeeded from people just looking at life, not as it is but as it could be.

Many of our children are born curious and ask the most ludicrous questions. That is in fact the birthplace of disruption. At first, ideas such as Uber, Airbnb, BuyPower, etc. seem outrightly amusing to ponder over until reality comes.

The next generation may have a list of skills that people need to have and your child should do well to keep up with it. Howbeit, you must continuously remind yourself that the future we anticipate is going to be created by disruptors who create the jobs of the future.

It is not a bad idea for your child to even consider being a disruptor.

5. **The Ikigai conversation**

Many parents are already overwhelmed with all this talk about entrepreneurship and innovation and perhaps purpose and fulfilment but they see far too many people struggle and families stranded because someone was pursuing a dream. They also see the seeming stability that comes with being gainfully employed.

The Ikigai conversation as captures in the image on the next page, is a word about helping people who want to create their own solutions to find a place of balance.

Ikigai

A JAPANESE CONCEPT MEANING "A REASON FOR BEING"

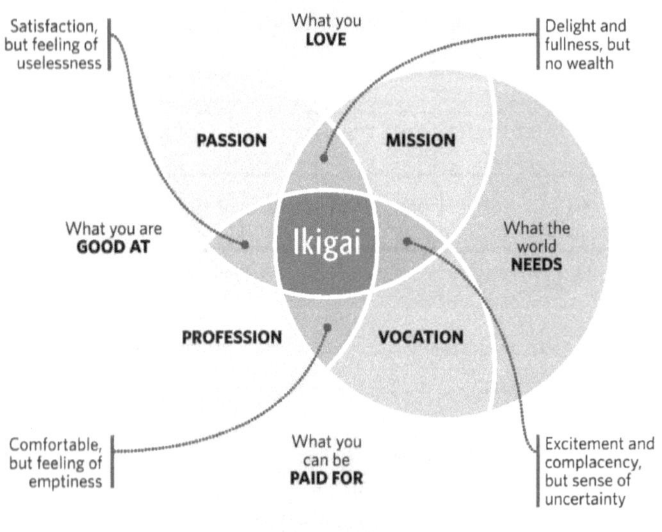

Ikigai talks about striking that delicate balance between what we are good at, what the world needs, what we love and what we can be paid for.

I sense that concern when teens and young people generally run off on their own to pursue an ideal life or some sort of utopia. It is at a point like this that the need to help them discover their Ikigai arises.

Have that conversation that enables them fine-tune their talents and what they love doing into commodities that can actually be paid for.

Again, It can serve as a resourcefulness task and decision-making if you ask them to design a blueprint for how they would make a living off what they do.

I want to assure you that with good thinking, there will always be a way. Please do not be dismissive just yet. Let me give you an example that you can use when having this conversation.

Let's say your son or daughter comes home with a fancy idea that you are really concerned about and they say they are passionate about it. Mention to the them that Bill Gates just 'loved' to code but still had to solve problems using his 'love' for coding. He had to find a way to turn around his passion to a corporate solution by creating products such as 'Windows" and "Microsoft packages,". So, ask them to show you a problem their passion solves as well as create products from it that people will be willing to pay for.

This helps us in several ways including helping parents who do not see possibilities outside of certain realities to unplug and appreciate the dynamism in the 21st century work space.

In addition, it will as well help young people to make objective decisions about work, rather than living in an utopia or forcing themselves into work realities they do not connect with.

Lessons that every 21st century child should learn from home.

What am about to share is what I actually use in my home. I call it the *21st Century Parenting Curriculum.* They are a list of values and concepts that I want to teach my children before they live home whether at 18 or 21.

The list is made up of 120 things but I am certain that you may have even more things to add to the list. This is because the list is in-exhaustive.

The **KNOSK** 21st Century Parenting Curriculum

- Africa / Nigeria and the Sustainable Development Goals (SDGs)
- Anger
- Appreciation
- Appreciating nature
- Being different
- Being led by The Spirit
- Body awareness
- Building with words
- Caring
- Choices
- Cleaning hacks.
- Conflict Resolution
- Contentment
- Courtesy
- Courage
- Creativity
- Death
- Democracy
- Determination
- Devotion
- Diligence
- Discipline
- Earning money
- Eating right
- Elections
- Empathy
- Etiquette (School, hospitality, social. dining etc.)

- Excellence
- Facing fear
- Fairness
- Faith
- Feeling disappointed
- Feeling sad
- Focus
- Foresight
- Forgiveness
- Friendship
- Frugal
- Full of the word
- Faithfulness
- Gentleness
- Goals
- Good Governance
- Goodness
- Great ideas
- Grit
- Growth
- Habits
- Hacks
- Helping
- Hope
- Hygiene
- Influence
- Initiative
- Innovation
- Insight
- Integrity
- Intuition
- Investing money
- Joy
- Keeping our words
- Keeping records
- Kindness
- Kitchen hacks
- Leadership
- Learning
- Love
- Loving family
- Loving God
- Loving others
- Loving yourself
- Maker hacks
- Making mistakes
- Media & entertainment
- Meeting people
- No pride
- Not quitting
- Optimism
- Passion
- Patience
- Peace
- Perseverance
- Perspective
- Planning
- Prayer
- Praying in tongues
- Problem solving
- Puberty
- Purpose
- Quantity of talk

- Reading
- Reaching out
- Resourcefulness
- Responsible Citizenship
- Respect
- Safety
- Saving money
- Self esteem
- Self confidence
- Self concept
- Self – Control
- Self respect
- Service
- Sex
- Sharing
- Speaking truth
- Sportsmanship
- Sympathy
- Talk-code
- Taking responsibility
- Teamwork
- Technology (Coding, cyber bullying, social - media)
- Tenacity
- Thinking
- Timeliness
- Travel
- Un-allowables
- Use of words
- Vision
- Volunteering

How do I plan to teach this?

<u>Step One:</u>

I want to first off talk about these concepts one after the other in such a way that I also answer my children's questions. Beginning with their immediate questions which would be about them getting clarity about what I am talking about. Essentially, answering their questions on meanings.

<u>Step Two;</u>
Afterwards, I want to answer their situational questions. This refers to questions that arise when they have thought through the concepts or experienced these concepts in their everyday life and they now have questions to ask.

<u>Step Three:</u>
Other than just talking and answering their questions, I want to model these concepts in my everyday experience. Meaning that, I would use them as personal guides as well.

<u>Step Four:</u>
Then I would go on to teach how-to.
This will include the right kind of thinking about these concepts as well as steps to take when
required to make a decision around these concepts.

<u>Step Five:</u>
I would also ask them to create their own ways of living out these concepts in ways that they can own beyond what I would teach them.

<u>Step Six:</u>
Another creative way to teach this is to ask older children to do research and then come back for everyone to have a discussion around the concepts.

These concepts will preserve children at school, at home, at work etc. These concepts would guide our children as they go into adults to make wholesome decisions, to live life fully and courageously etc.

Seeing that they are about 120, how should a parent teach all of this?

We should all have a way we want to do this. There is no one way to do this. Choose what works best for you.
Below are a few ways you can try, but like I said, you do not necessarily need to follow these ways;

<u>Idea One:</u>
Personally, I have all these words hung up in my room and I ask my daughters to point at any word, pronounce them or attempt to pronounce them and I would be right there to start the conversation.

Usually for weeks on end, situations will arise either between the girls, or from something on TV or something we observe in a public place or something they teach them at church or school and we loop it back to the conversation. Usually, it doesn't take long before I hear the girls begin to talk about it to themselves.
The downside of this approach is that it may be inconsistent and children can ask about more than one concept and muddle it all up.

<u>Idea Two:</u>
I have also heard a parent coach say, she does something similar as word of the week or word of the month   or   so.

If you have pre-teens, I recommend doing one word each month. If you have teens aged 13-15 or there about you can do one word every two weeks.

And if you have children 16-18 who would soon be living home, you can have a weekly one night out where you talk about one concept for each week.

<u>Idea Three:</u>
Write out these words in a flash card and leave them in a box for one child to take at the beginning of the week or the beginning of the month.
Let them take turns to pick this flash cards.

You can then make copies of the word and leave them in strategic places to keep the conversation going. If you can, stick up words that you have concluded on, on a particular wall so that we can look up and see what we   have   learned   so   far.

<u>Idea Four:</u>
You can pick 12 themes a year and it will be fine. It is absolutely okay to take between 10 - 15 years to cover this exhaustively if you have younger children. Some concepts like 'sex' will be taught over and over in age appropriate ways as children grow up.

In the course of teaching this, you would find that, reading helps. As your children read books, you have loads of scenarios to use when having these conversations. Sometimes, you would run into books that have these themes in stories. It can be a great tool for expanding the children's knowledge base on themes as well as yours.

- **Key Points**

- The 21st century is actually the best time to have the job of your dreams.
- Today, children can have access to all the knowledge, information and skill building opportunities that they need.
- While it is important to prepare children for employment, it is also crucial to prepare them to venture out on their own and be employers of labour.
- Before dismissing, your son or daughter's idealism, ask them to, from what they love doing, create products that people would be willing to buy.

#11 COMMUNICATION: THE POWER TOOL OF 21ST CENTURY PARENTING

Communication remains the most powerful tool for parenting.

In the face of changes, fluid influences and several things contending for attention, communication is the meat of parenting. It is the backbone for handling your responsibility as a parent.

In times past, our parents threw words around carelessly. They had a right to speak as they liked, we had no right on the other hand to even feel bad let alone talking back. Now, we know better. For one, we know that we create our world with our words and our words to our children become the building blocks of their sense of worth.

How does communication aid parenting?
Communication is the tool through which our children learn about who we are and what is important or not important to us.

Parenting is how we voice our fears, concerns, standards, etc.

Our children learn about us through the words we speak to them, about them, about ourselves, others and things generally.

Through communication, we shape our children's beliefs. We empower or disempower. We give them wings or we clip their wings.

It is also the mechanism through which we inspire positive actions in our children. When we praise, complement, say kind words, we enable our children to take the steps. I know how many times, I have heard my children say to each other, "you can do this."

At other times, I have even heard them call out their own names and say to themselves, "I can do this."

Peggy O'mara's quote captures it perfectly. She says, "The way we talk to our children becomes their inner voice."

Communication aids modeling. We can model respect, faith, care, kindness through our words. We can instruct with our words as to what we require of our children.

Communication Skills That Every Parent Must Imbibe

Contemporary parents need to incorporate a number of qualities into their communication to make their interaction with their children effective.

These are discussed below.

1.   Clarity

There is good and bad communication in parenting. Good communication leads a child to take the desired action. Bad communication leaves a child with insufficient knowledge as to what actions they are expected to take. This means that when we have communicated right, a child should know clearly what he or she is expected to do.

We can usually clarify this by asking the child to repeat what we said.

We are also supposed to use few simple words as well as breakdown expectations as a whole into simple concepts.

For instance, go and have a bath may be a bit complex for your four to six year olds. Instead, giving bite-sized instructions like put on your slippers, go brush your teeth, etc., may help them perform small-sized actions that move them towards the goal.

2.   Listening

This is a concept that the average adult needs to learn to better our everyday life experiences. When it comes to parenting, listening is where we demonstrate the highest form of validation for our children.

Listening involves showing interest in the things that are important to our children. Keeping our phone down, maintaining eye contact, nodding, asking questions, smiling or showing the appropriate emotions for the moment are all part of listening.

However, the crux is to actually listen. It is not just about making facial expressions or being conscious of how we want our children to feel during conversations but actually involves showing genuine interest and seeking to understand the child and what they are saying.

Listening means we will be able to notice our children's choice of words (which can reveal things they are not talking about), their body language and the point they are trying to make.

3.   Speak to your audience
First, this speaks of context and tonality. When speaking, speak in a manner that your child understands.

Use examples and scenarios that your child can relate with. Speak to each child in the way they can relate.

Our children are different and will respond to things differently.

So, communication needs to be tailored to address each child's approach. Generally, it is recommended to squat or sit in order to speak at eyeball to eyeball levels.

Towering over children affects communication as the process of looking up at us, causes discomfort and distorts messaging.

4.   Friendliness
Our tone of communicating with our children must be from a place of friendliness. We must uphold our children. We will only be able to correct our children effectively when they accept us or perceive us as being after their best interest. We can only earn this from maintaining a loving disposition when interacting with them.

5.   Empathy
The truth about parenting is that your children at different ages of their lives will make a big deal about something that is totally unimportant to you but obviously not to them. Patience and empathy are crucial in those moments.

Showing empathy begins with being sensitive to our children and choosing words deliberately even when we think that what they are worried about is not important. Usually, from a child's point of view, those things are important.

When a parent demonstrates empathy, they show the child respect for their views even while helping them make adjustments and at the same time create room for earning respect.

Modeling is a great parenting tool and the way we speak to our children becomes the way they will speak to themselves, their siblings and eventually to us.

6.	Emotional Intelligence

This is simply defined as the capacity to be aware of, control, and express one's emotions, and to handle interpersonal relationships judiciously and empathetically. Today's parents are overwhelmed to the core. Fatigue seems to be eating away at our core. It is so easy to yell at simple mistakes that our children should be expected to make. The fatigue impairs our judgment and enables us do more harm than good to our children.

There are some underlying truths about yelling that we should know.

First, yelling does not make what we are saying to the children clearer. Yelling is an expression of anger. The first question is to ask, "What am I angry at?" If your child did wrong, could it be a time to create a teachable moment? Could it be a time to clarify?

Research shows that yelling leads to more and more behavior problems. "Children are actually going to listen less when you yell at them," says Joseph Shrand, Ph.D., instructor of psychiatry at Harvard Medical School. "As soon as you begin to raise your voice, you activate their limbic system, which is an ancient part of the brain that's responsible for, among other things, the fight-or-flight response."

Children who have been raised with harsh verbal discipline are at increased risk to develop anxiety, depression, and behavioral problems, according to the results of research cited by Mandy Velez in the Sept 6, 2013 Parents ("Yelling at Children Could be Just as Harmful as Physical Discipline, Study Suggests").

It's time to put our emotions and expectations together and embrace the concept that as parents, we are first teachers. We teach, repeat, evaluate and we need to be patient enough while teaching in order to stop emotions from getting in the way.

We can start by creating clear standards that the children are familiar with. These standards must be clear enough for everyone to understand. The accompanying rewards and consequences must also be known, so that there is no need to make on-the-spot decisions. Thus, allowing you to take some time and calm down.

Taking time out allows you to be more objective while also reducing the tendency for your child to be defensive and not in a state of mind to learn from what you would say.

7.   Understand non-verbal cues
While speaking with your children, pay attention to note when they do not understand what you are saying, so that you do not waste your time and feel drained thinking that you have been communicating. Effective communication may not be possible when a child is fearful, tired, hungry and restless.

- Key Points

- We create our world with our words and our words to our children become the building blocks to their sense of worth.
- Through communication we model the beliefs, values and standards we want our children to uphold.
- Listening is how we demonstrate the highest form of validation for our children.
- There is good communication, bad communication and no communication.

#12 TO SPANK OR NOT TO SPANK

This is the 21st century obviously and you cannot speak or write about parenting without the subject of spanking being brought up. There are many schools of thought that continue to look at the subject from a human rights point of view. Most of the research carried out in this regard, have been conducted outside of the African soil.

Humans are essentially the same everywhere in my opinion and if studies are coming up, saying that spanking has an undesirable effect on our children, rather than just dismiss them, it may be good for us to conduct researches in our clime and see what the outcomes directly tell us.

I recall my mother telling me as a child that we were blacks and having absent fathers had no impact.

I disagreed with her and told her it did, because I was black and yet every time I thought about or there was a mention of anything close to fatherhood it elicited a unique set of emotions within me. So, I can say that the average African lives in denial. Motives may differ but usually, we are afraid to confront hard held concepts for fear of what we would be without them.

Perhaps, if we could do our own research and explore our own context, not only would we establish the impact of spanking on our children, but we would also learn how best our children would respond and what discipline is effective or not.

This section of the book focuses on my own thoughts about spanking my children. A few years ago, I would readily spank my children in the face of misbehavior but sitting through what I was trying to achieve, I had to rethink the whole thing.

First, we want to shape behavior. To shape behavior, I need to provide information in a way that the child sees that it's for their own good. Sometime their own good should not be about what I would do to them but for their own self-respect.

My child should not steal because of what I will do to them, but because of what stealing will do to them. How people will shame them, look down on them is perhaps more compelling than what I would do. What if I am not around? What if I never get to know? Who should my children be?

Second, I would spank my child and then say I did it because I loved them. Wouldn't that be distorted when a spouse hits them, says he loves them and I disagree? Isn't that what I modeled to them? Is it remotely possible to compartmentalize like that? Maybe, maybe not.

Some western views appear permissive to me. They sound like a child is wired to know their way around life. I am the guide, I will be firm just that I realize that besides the fact that spanking may not be a safe tool to use, it also is not the only tool available for discipline. I have seen my peers whose parents nearly killed while flogging them and how it had almost no effect on their behavior but rather turned them into very cold people.

My daughters who are 7 and 5 hold a different view. They say that when I spank them, they were filled with remorse and asked themselves why they did this in the first place. I believe it is because of the relationship and rapport that we have built, owing to the fact that during those moments, they actually miss the moments we spend together and so, the regret is based on their desire to have their mummy back.

What about cases where parents have no relationship vault for which children can see through to their motives of providing correction?

But again, learning is far more important than having their mummy back. They can feign remorse just so that we keep things moving.

Spanking may indeed stop children at that moment, but research shows that in the long run, pain and fear can prevent children from learning the lessons the parents are trying to teach them. "Spanking doesn't teach children to behave the way parents want them to, and can have the opposite effect," says Dr. Gershoff. "Children who are hit are often compliant immediately, but they haven't been taught how to be better in the long term." "Hitting doesn't teach them why what they did was wrong or what they should do next time," says Dr. Gershoff, a developmental psychologist and associate professor at the Department of Human Development and Family Science at the University of Texas at Austin.

Spanking teaches children how to avoid being hit instead of helping them develop positive motivations for good behavior.

Some children have turned around to become so timid and very inexpressive as a result.

So, as a Nigerian mum, raising daughters, I am asking myself what is the most strategic way to go about this business of shaping behavior? What other ways are there that may be more effective and without the possibility of unhealthy long-term consequences?

1.   Start with a belief
Create a family identity that you uphold that will get your children so proud to be a part of; a family that models sanity and responsibility.

Sell that idea to your children. For Instance, we are kind to each other, we are respectful of each other, and we love each other. Imagine a family whose core is that love lives here. Children feel accepted and parents model that they are important.

Children themselves can oftentimes remind each other of the values when they act in ways that are not consistent.

2.   Give everybody the opportunity to grow
Sometimes we have adult expectations on children. Let us avail them the opportunity to learn, make mistakes and grow.

Asking a child to redo a task until they get it is far more effective than spanking them and asking them to go to bed or spanking them and asking them to redo. In my opinion, while the former is totally pointless, in doing the former, coordination and learning will be significantly undermined.

3.   Cultivate a close-knit relationship with your children that allows you all talk freely including sharing your expectations of each other.

My daughters can easily tell me to my face that we have not had our usual conversations.

During these book writing projects, while spending time with the girls, one of them got teary and when I asked why, she said we had not spoken for weeks the way we did that night and went further to tell me how she missed it.

This kind of close relationship can inspire a child to be in their best behavior in order to not go against a parent and foul the atmosphere. They cherish times spent with us and they can usually translate this friendship to a willingness to live out family standards. Not also leaving out that they usually understand what we are trying to achieve and can hold siblings accountable to set standards.

The relationship makes it possible for parents and children to talk through areas of concerns and ambiguity.

4.   Make challenging times, opportunities for building relationship, learning and upholding values.

Just about any parent knows that challenging times are those moments when our children misbehave and go against what we may have taught them or expect from them. It is during these times that we really face the core of choosing between spanking or more wholesome approaches.

There are different reasons why children misbehave. Here are a few of them and alternative ways to discipline them other than spanking:

Children misbehave because they are not aware of clearly set standard

Yes, many times our children behave in certain ways because we have not expressly set the standard and they do not understand what they should do or not do. As parents, we unconsciously tell our children "stop," "do not do that" without necessarily providing the alternative activity.

For instance, a better way to put it could be, "do not stand in front of the TV, sit here instead." Also, sometimes taking out the negative command completely and sticking with the expected instruction has a stronger impact.

So, you can totally do away with, "stop" and "do not" and rather say, "Leave there and come sit here."

<u>Children misbehave because we are not consistent and firm</u>
This is a situation in which one day, we have a particular standard and another day we let it pass. This way, we end up creating the impression that we are not very serious about our standards.

When you give in to their emotional blackmail, they will consider the misbehavior effective and continue. Some children pester until you give in. becoming aware of the approach equips you to deal with the misbehavior objectively.

<u>Children will be children</u>

Our children will make mistakes, some very costly. Sometimes it will be as a result of ignorance, lapse in judgment or carelessness.

Knowing which is which is most important for shaping behavior, so that we address issues appropriately.

I have used demonstration as a post-misbehavior tool. That is, showing the child what to do another time. If it's a lapse in judgment, we talk through what they considered and what they did not and if it's out of carelessness, I am available for a do over.

Moments of misbehavior offer us a rare opportunity to teach our children new problem-solving skills. Whether it is with how they manage anger, excitement or new experiences, in those moments where they fall short, we can open a door of learning and of growth.

<u>Children misbehave because their context may not have been completely captured in the rule.</u>

This applies for all ages.
When rules are narrow without consideration for the different contexts a child may be in, they can create room for misbehavior. The misbehavior may be out of not understanding what to do in a certain context.

Let's say you have a bedtime rule that says that bedtime is for 8pm but you do not consider if a child had napped in the afternoon and woke up at 7pm and is not sleepy. All efforts to send the child to bed will be met with resistance. At the same time, we can not leave the child to wander until midnight. So we create an alternative window that says what bedtime is in this new context.

Also, discussing rules with your children in a way that makes them contribute to the decision-making process enables buy-in as well as accurate recollection of what the rule is.
<u>Many children misbehave because we do not have clear rewards and consequence systems.</u>

Many times, when this is the case, we sermonize when children misbehave instead of firmly allowing the consequences to pan out, we shout, we yell and the child faces no consequence. Whenever we yell and are so upset, what we are doing is punishing ourselves for the child's misbehavior.

You can use natural and logical consequences and you can create other consequences.

Natural consequences follow the natural cause of life and require no human interference. For example, if you poured it, clean it up. If you left your school bag at school, then you will face the disciplinary measure of not doing your homework. I will not be worked up on your behalf.

I recall this dance recital the girls had to go for. I had mentioned that they should pack up their bags and all they needed. They got excited and by the time we got to the venue which was about a 35 minutes ride from the house, we discovered one of them had left her underwear for the dance.

She ran to me and whispered, "Mummy, please can you go home to bring me my black tights?" and I whispered back "it's too far from here. If I went, the presentation will be completely done before I would get back here."

Her dance instructor asked her to make do with her school short which was not as comfortable in the routines. She believed she performed far less than par but took an important lesson that no matter how excited you are thoughtfulness was still required. No fights, no fuss, lessons learnt, happy space, high chance of a better choice another time!

A logical consequence on the other hand is what we have designed to make life sane at home. If you have a child who loves to do something that puts everyone else at risk, then together, we can all agree on something that can be taken from him so that he experiences a similar discomfort.

So, a child who forgot to put away his Gamebox console after playing his game can go 2-3 days without the game to learn that if he needs to play this, then he needs to take good care of things.

These consequences have to be pre-planned so that on the day you come home from work and you are in the realm of very poor judgment, the child himself will know to pack up the Gamebox console and bring it to your room. No noise. The child already knows what the deal is.

No fuss.

In summary, consequences remove the need to exert emotions and allow the child take responsibility seeing that he or she can connect their own actions to where they are. Consequences give children the power to choose an outcome of choice.

What about using rewards?
Designing rewards, like consequences is effective when they are pre-planned, so that we do not over-reward or under-reward. In the process of creating a reward system, ensure your children contribute ideas to what the rewards should be. That way, the rewards are actually some things they look forward to.

Whenever many parents hear rewards, it appears they see themselves buying ice cream or spending money. Those are not the only kinds of rewards.

There are simpler, richer, bond building rewards like "give a dramatic hi-5," "no chores day," etc. They do not cost money per se but can he used to measure and reward children for milestones they achieve

Other disciplinary tools can be explored including 'restitution' which is a type of logical consequence that makes a child pay back for wrongs they did. For example, if they said something mean to a sibling or a classmate, they will be required to come up with three really nice things to say as a consequence. If they spilled water on the floor, for example, they would be required to mop.

6. Children misbehave because they need attention

Yes, sometimes it could be because they are hungry, agitated, lonely and tired, especially in younger children. In older children, they may be hurting and trying to get you to notice so that you come to a place where you can privately talk.

As a 21st century parent, you should train your senses to know when the child really needs you. One cue I recommend for parents to always use is to learn about our children on a personal level. Know your child. If a child who hardly uses a swear word suddenly does, then, something is off. Call that child in and talk.

Generally, children of different ages have distinct needs. Sometimes as parents when we are not quick to understand the peculiar need of each age group, we tend to box them into realities they do not connect with. For instance, bathroom routines can become a bore when your 5-year-old begins to think that they can bathe themselves. Sometimes, the response is to empower them with the new liberty or independence they want to explore while guiding them.

153

- **Key Points**

- Spanking is one of the least effective tools for disciplining.
- Parents ought to pay attention to the causes of misbehavior so that it can be addressed from the root.
- Many times we have unrealistic expectations for our children. Children would be children.
- Our primary goal is to teach. Teaching needs to be done repeatedly, patiently and through effective communication.
- It will always be easier for parents who have a beautiful relationship with their children, to get across to them and correct them.

154

**THE CRUX OF THE MATTER: BUILDING EMOTIONAL RESILIENCE

The reason I wrote many things I have written in the previous parts of this book was to bring me to the place where I could get to talk about how today, children essentially lacks emotional resilience. They cry and break down at correction and sometimes are completely oblivious of how one action they take could impact another person. They live in a world of their own.

This can be very frustrating for parents, who realized that their own parents never even paid attention to see if they were upset or not. It appears as though we were able to shake it off. But did we? Or we could muster courage and pretend that everything was great if not another layer of spanking.

Have you ever stopped to wonder why our children do not greet? Sometimes I like to believe that our box-type way of raising children where the entertainment and fun and everything else happens within a few cubic meters of their life with zero to no interaction with the outside world other than when they go to school, church or mosque, could be responsible.

So first, they lack emotional resilience; which I believe comes from a place where they believe their own thoughts too quickly. They think wrong and they run with it.

There are not enough holistic adult conversations happening around them. The number of adults who model what the benchmark for accepting what they believe should be is not sufficient.

This particular responsibility lies on parents and grandparents. The non-parental care givers have the primary responsibility of getting the children through the day. Ensuring they wash up, eat, do their homework, etc. They will be unable to feed the minds of our children. In other words, we will teach them to uphold standards but they do not have access to what our children are thinking.

The high suicide rates and depression are coming from this place of wrong thinking. You do not also fight about wrong thinking; you replace them with the right thoughts. In my home, I call it "truths."

So when one of my children has a countenance that shows that something is not right, I ask them what they are thinking. I may ask other questions but the core for me is to have them voice their thoughts. You cannot scold a child to share their thoughts. You must have a rapport that makes them talk freely without thinking they would look stupid or be scolded.

I would usually ask, after I heard what they said, is that the truth? Is this thought consistent with what you have been told, taught or previous incidents relating to the particular issue they are talking about. And then we will break down the conversation.

Let me give a typical scenario. One morning, my second was trying to change from her pajamas to another set of clothes before having a bath. She picked up this really nice top and I asked her to pick another and keep it until she had showered.

It was the second top she had picked and I had thought it was inappropriate for wearing before they had bathe.

Then her countenance fell. It didn't take long for tears to start gathering in the cloud. So, I called her to sit beside me and tell me what she was thinking. And then the following conversations ensued:

Daughter: Mummy, I am feeling very bad.

Irene: Hmmm, why?

Daughter: You keep saying No to me. You keep saying No to me!

Irene: (Pet name), these clothes you picked are really nice. But you would be bathing in about one hour. After bathing, they will have to go to the laundry. But if you wear any of them after you bathe you would wear it for longer.

Daughter: (Her face lights up because new thinking is introduced)

Some background, when she thought I was saying No was because I first started out by saying to her that one of them was too light and it was cold in the morning. But she came up with the idea that she will wear a long sleeve under it. Great, right? But mummy still said No.

This generation is not playing in the sand outside to make resilient, self-protective decisions like we used to. They faint easily.

Our responsibility is to start by arming them with stable thoughts.

I have seen my children faint, as in fall flat emotionally, while being corrected for something that they did like not greeting in the morning. And they will feel a mixture of emotions that you will be wondering where it came from.

While children must be allowed to think and feel, wrong unresolved thoughts become mind-sets that shape actions and expectations.

I have heard children whose parents were doing their very best for say they are not loved. And if they say this long enough, they believe it, resent their parents and become susceptible to all kind of people that would hurt them.

In my home, I have taught them and we have discussed repeatedly that corrections are teachings. I used the school example the other day, that we learn more after a failure. If you failed to get an answer right in a test, during the correction you got the opportunity to learn it over. In the end, you would know more. So, I tell them correction makes them better people.

And to manage the immediate foul mood, they say a one sentence affirmation which is, "I take corrections easily and happily."

On anti-social behaviors, parents need to put their children in pro-social situations. Take them to your office periodically and send them to help you go to people to do or get something. In those processes, they learn the intricacies of social relationships.

When foster children are going on errands to buy things for the house, within walking distances in the area, from those little corner shops and all, let them go with them.

Take them on walks, on visits to neighbors and organize play dates with friends and family. Let them interact with other people other than people from their immediate family.

This should be encouraged because the relationships they have at school are somehow regimented and their level of demonstrating pro-social behavior is different when they are in really open space. Have your children answer the house phone where they have to speak to people with respect, listen, get information and share their thoughts while putting emotions in place.

Let them welcome and serve guests when they come around. They need to be taught to shake hands firmly, hug, maintain eye contact, exchange pleasantries and ask what they can do to make the guest comfortable. If the guests come with children, they need to lead the children to where they can play and ensure the children are comfortable.

Finally, we need to raise children who have a disposition to protect themselves and are alert. We have not yet been put in an awkward situation where the children needed to bail themselves out but we have been where other people tried to bully them and they did not speak up enough for themselves.

The other time, one of my daughters at school, had a boy trashing her art work and she came home and asked me to speak to the boy. When her teacher was trashing the art, I reached out to him but now it was her peer. I needed her to learn to stand up for what she wanted.

So, I asked her, why she had a problem with him trashing her art. And she told me that her art was important to her. So, I asked her to let her classmate know that it was important to her. Needless to say, that was the end of the art trashing episode.

Part of our work is to raise strong children who cannot be bullied and do not bully others. Children who, in the face of any threatening situation, will know when to speak up, talk to a person in authority and even walk away.

I am proactively teaching my children to voice their thought. Charity begins at home. If we do not want them to be intimidated out there, they must be comfortable expressing their views from home.

During the last Christmas holiday, the children needed casual sandals. I had decided to buy crocs for them. I took them along. The moment we got to the shop, my second daughter said she could not wear the crocs. The countenance of my first dropped but she said she could manage a particular one.

Then I called them out of the store and said, "You have to say what you mean and mean what you say. If you are not comfortable about something speak up."

I have raised my children to not want everything they see but I still need them to voice their opinions. I seized the opportunity to explain to them that mummy or daddy does not need to do everything you ask for, but speaking up makes them become aware of what you think and that consideration would usually be made. We ended up picking another set of casual shoes that were not crocs.

We need to teach and assure our children that their views and thoughts will be heard and so they must speak up. If we shut our children down at home, then they will come to believe that their voices or opinions never count.

What can happen as a result is that even in moments of emergency or where someone who has no jurisdiction tries to abuse them, they would have no courage to fight back. And another outcome could be outright rebellion.

To forestall this, I encourage my children to say what they feel and what they expect.

I also encourage them to negotiate. There would be rules and consequences and they should not be tested. But I do not want them to feel like having cereal but are concerned with whether they would get approval.

There have been times I have told them the foster children have closed for the day and should not be disturbed. But I have gone further to teach them how to make their own cereal and beverage drinks.

I have made the effort to ask for their opinion and plans and when they have asked for things we could not do, I have told them we will consider it in the future.

I encourage them to ask questions when they begin to think in a particular way. Asking "do you mean" questions to address their thoughts and concerns helps get the right information to them.

For instance, when I told one of my daughters that she could not wear those tops that morning, if she had a thought that said "mummy said no because she is mad at me or she does not want me to wear the clothes I like",

I expect her to ask me straight away. I would expect her to ask me if my actions mean that I am mad at her or that I do not want her to wear the clothes she loves. This is it. Rather than going away with wrong thinking and all, I encourage them to ask questions to clarify their thoughts.

So many adults today are struggling in this area. They hardly ever share what they truly mean. They are far too fixated on saying what they believe the listener wants to hear. While some other have an outburst because of meanings they ascribe to other people's facial expression, words and other things.

The 21st century parent cannot be as dismissive as his or her parents were. He or she must in all sincerity and objectivity, correct the misconceptions of past generations and essentially move towards raising wholesome beings.

- **Key Points**

- Listen.

- Encourage your children to air their views.

- Run a pro-knowledge and pro-thinking space. Expand your children's knowledge and perspectives, and then create an atmosphere that encourages deep thinking over hasty conclusions.

- Steadily put your children in situations that encourage interaction with adults and children alike.

- All of the above will help your children build emotional resilience.

166

CONCLUSION

Contrary to what our own parents say, we do not have it easier as parents today. Just because we have phones, the internet and TV, does not mean we have it easier. The peculiarity of our times in itself brings along its own fair share of challenges.

As a parent today, you realize how delicate a time it is to raise children. The mere thought that what you do or do not do will have an impact on someone else's life is such a reminder that we must not do guess work or trial and errors. Neither should we try out what our parents did.

We can draw from their principles but we have to be creative in approach.

Like I mentioned at the beginning, this town is a whole different city from the one you were raised in. You cannot just throw around your childhood sentiments.

This city needs hard proof of what really works and not just old wives' tales. You cannot ignore what is in your face. To navigate this city and get the best out of it, you need to know what fuels and drives this city.

What the cries are? What the sentiments are? Why they fight easily? Why they have their tongues out? What the obsession with selfies is about?

But more than knowing you need to be present and connect.

We have shared an evidence-based conversation, from researches to opinions and personal journeys. In these lines, I believe I have touched some questions and thoughts you have had but may not have spoken about them.

Take what is in here and run with it. Personalize it. Add some of your own spice. You can do this.

ABOUT THE AUTHOR

Irene Bangwell is the Co-founder of KNOSK, an education innovation company that focuses on actionizing learning, education research and providing parenting education.

She writes, creates new tools, and designs programs that make learning spaces more empowering for children and teens. She is the designer of the Education Innovation Map, amongst other education management tools.

Irene Bangwell has authored other parenting books including; **Raising Children Who Are Influence Proof, Moving from Overwhelmed to Overwhelm, Back2School Success Kit** and **Raising Girls and the Boys who would love them.**

She has worked as an on-air parenting coach since 2010 and has mentored and continues to mentor hundreds of teens since 2008.

Irene Bangwell is married to Kingsley Bangwell and together they have two amazing daughters, Briona and Elena who love God, arts and want to solve global problems.

To learn more about KNOSK;
Visit: www.knoskeducation.com
Email: ask@knosk.com.ng
Phone: +234 9033338510.